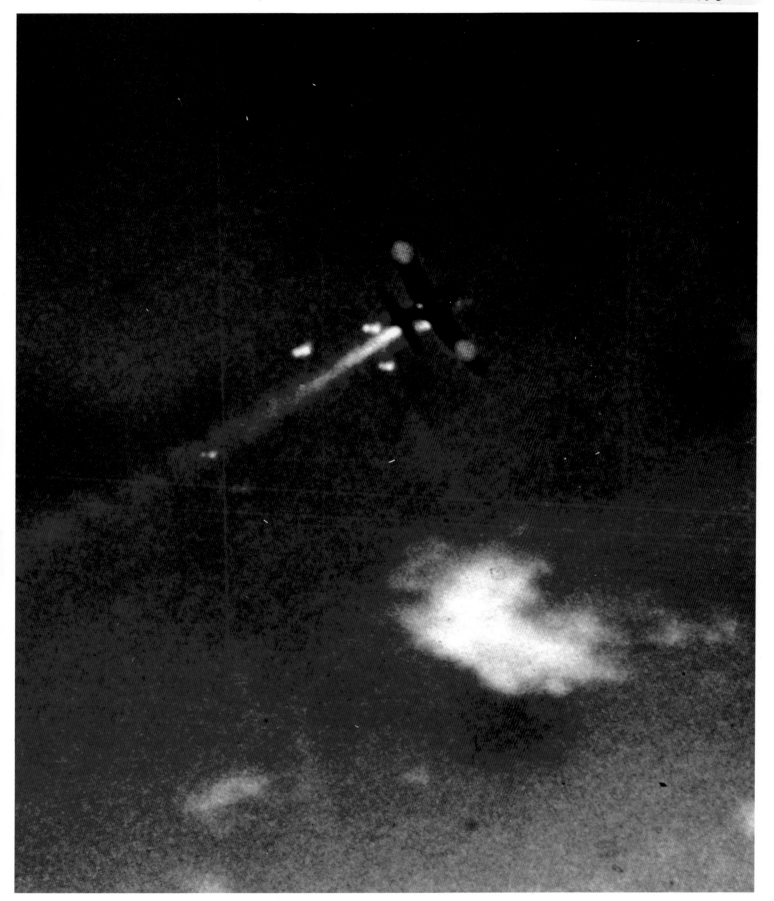

Motorbooks International
WARBIRD HISTORY

ZERO

Robert C. Mikesh
Foreword by Japanese Zero Ace Saburo Sakai

First published in 1994 by Motorbooks International Publishers & Wholesalers, PO Box 2, 729 Prospect Avenue, Osceola, WI 54020 USA

Motorbooks International books are also available at discounts in bulk quantity for industrial or sales-promotional use. For details write to Special Sales Manager at the Publisher's address

Library of Congress Cataloging-in-Publication Data Available

ISBN 0-87938-915-X

On the front cover: *A Mitsubishi Zero A6M2 from the early Pacific War era, now restored and flown by the Confederate Air Force. This is one of only two Zeros that is currently flyable. It was piloted on this occasion by Dr. John Kelley.* Brian M. Silcox

On the frontispiece page: *Gun camera footage of a Zero's demise. National Archives*

On the title page: *Dr. John Kelly brings the Confederate Air Force Zero in for landing.* Brian Silcox

On the back cover: *A Zero A6M5 on roll-out after restoration at Johnson (now Iruma) AB in 1963. This Zero is currently owned by the JASDF and is based at Hamamatsu AB, Japan.* **Inset photo:** *Cockpit of the A6M5 owned by the National Air & Space Museum. This plane was captured by Americans on Saipan during World War II.* Robesrt C. Mikesh

Printed and bound in Hong Kong

Contents

Foreword

I began flying the Zero Fighter when it was first called the Experimental 12-*Shi* Carrier Fighter. This began for me in mid-1940. Over the many years since that time, I can proudly look back upon the operational years of the Zero Fighter and know that I was fully involved from its infancy to the end of its combat career.

In the early part of the Zero's development, performance tests were conducted against other fighters that were in use at that time. The most important challenger in this comparison testing with the Zero was the Mitsubishi A5M Navy Type 96 Carrier Fighter (Allied code named Claude). The Japanese Navy was extremely proud of this aircraft in that it was an exceptional fighter. I became involved in these flight tests as well. Test results showed that the Zero was inferior to the Claude in many aspects. As such, the Type 96 Carrier Fighter was an excellent single-seat fighter that was particularly superior in dogfights. However, the Zero was officially selected as the next generation naval fighter. The deciding factors were the Zero's incredible range (more than twice that of the Type 96) and the increased firepower with upgraded weapons. And, of course, the Zero was considered to have far greater maneuverability than any other fighter of advanced nations.

This decision proved correct on the thirteenth of September 1940 during its combat debut over China. Long-distance offensives that had been impossible with the Type 96 Carrier Fighter now became a reality with the Zero Fighter. While escorting a bomber force, 13 Zeros flew from the Japanese base at Hankow to Chungking, a distance of 485 statute miles one-way. Over that city, they encountered 27 Chinese fighters (Polikarpov I-15 and I-16), shot them all down, and returned to their base at Hankow without a loss.

I flew the Zero in early operations in China, as well as on the opening day of the Pacific war and long thereafter. My wingmen and I engaged in many air battles and dominated the skies. When I flew the Zero in combat, I always felt like my aircraft and myself were one. It was just like riding a fine horse in the way an old equestrian term describes horsemanship–the rider and his horse are one. I felt as if the tip of the propeller spinner was the middle of my forehead and the wing tips were the tips of my middle fingers with my arms extended.

However, the Zero, too, was not almighty. Its fantastic maneuverability was excellent only at the lower and medium flying speeds. In August 1943, the US forces introduced the Grumman F6F Hellcat and North American P-51 Mustang into the arena. They had more horsepower, better high-speed maneuverability, and increased firepower. This took away the legendary invincibility for air superiority of the Zero Fighter in the Pacific.

Above 250kt air speed, the Zero could not respond quickly due to the increased air loads on its flight controls, and pilots could not adequately overcome this. Furthermore, our hastily trained replacement pilots' skill and overall ability to fight was much less than those of the pilots before them. Japan's inferiority in firepower and sheer numbers of aircraft available against the Allied power, determined victory or defeat in battle. Regardless of this fact, veteran Japanese pilots who fought throughout the war were still confident that they could always win if they were flying a Zero one-on-one against any Allied fighter. In other words, the outcome of any air battle depended upon the pilot's skill, not on the type of aircraft.

In retrospect, I now realize that the Zero was best only for attack, regardless of the intent of its design at the time. The Zero's extremely lightweight construction was the result of its weak airframe. This brought about an obvious fear in the minds of the pilots that flew the Zero, particularly while in a dive and picking up speed. In addition to this, the Zero had no self-sealing fuel tanks nor armor plating to protect the pilot.

It took the Japanese attitude of a *Samurai* warrior to overcome these weaknesses. Nevertheless, the Zero Fighters and their pilots fought nobly. The power of Zero Fighters as a group was extremely forceful and the Zero was once a truly supreme ruler of the Pacific skies.

If the Zero had never been designed or produced, the Japanese Navy would not have decided to initiate the Pacific war. Many Japanese believe this theory even today.

The *Reisen* (Zero Fighter) will live on in the hearts of the Japanese people forever.

Saburo Sakai

Saburo Sakai, Japan's leading surviving Zero ace.

Preface

Although no one knew at its inception, Saburo Sakai's "fine horse" of an airplane would one day become known to the world as the famous—or infamous—Zero Fighter, depending upon which direction its guns were pointed! To the unfamiliar, the term Zero, meaning nothing, was a strange title to bestow upon an airplane that was to have such world impact. When the name was first discovered by intelligence personnel, it was equally as puzzling then as it is today.

This legendary name came from its official title, which in English was the Mitsubishi Navy Type Zero Carrier-Based Fighter. Beginning in the late 1920s, both the Japanese Army and Navy used type numbers based upon the last two digits of the Japanese national era system calendar, which retroactively was set at 660 BC, the founding date of the Japanese State. The Zero Fighter was given the Type number *Rei,* meaning "Zero," when it was accepted by the Navy in their year of 2600, which coincides with 1940. With the turn of that decade, the Navy changed to using just the last single digit for their type numbers and the Army followed suit a year later.

So when stated in Japanese, the airplane became *Rei Shiki Sentoki* (Type Zero Fighter), normally shortened to the abbreviation of *Rei-sen* or *Reisen.* Without question, this word identified the Mitsubishi fighter, even though there were seven other Type Zero aircraft, but of different missions stated in their service titles. The popularity of this designation to this particular airplane became so great that even the Japanese after World War II adopted the Americanized *Zero-sen* or *Zero Fighter.*

The entire and often changing designation system of Japanese Army and Navy aircraft was never fully understood by Allied intelligence during the war years. The inability to properly and quickly identify aircraft types for the Allied aircrews made the task of defense difficult. To help solve the problem, a simple, easy to remember code-name system was developed. Male names were given to fighters and floatplanes; female names were given to bombers, reconnaissance aircraft, and flying boats. In the case of the *Zero-sen,* the name Zeke was assigned, but by this time the term Zero was indelibly popular and was more often used than Zeke. In fact, the Zero became so well publicized at the opening phase of the war that even today, people often identify nearly any low-wing radial-engine fighter having a Japanese insignia as a Zero, regardless of its type.

The use of "Zero" as a blanket term for Japanese fighters derives from mistaken identity between the Japanese Army and Navy. The Zero was—and is today—often confused with the Army's Nakajima Ki-43 Hayabusa, code named Oscar by the Allies. The Oscar was developed a year after the Zero, yet had basically the same engine and very similar appearance. Allied aviators in China and in the Southwest Pacific Area (SPA) frequently reported contacts with Zeros when the planes they met were actually Oscars. To compound the case, Allied intelligence thought the Zero was possibly operated by both the Japanese Army Air Force (JAAF) and Japanese Naval Air Force (JNAF), this confusion having arisen out of the fact that a large number of land-based naval air units shared bases with Army air units in the island campaigns of the Southwest Pacific. The JAAF did not use the Zero Fighter.

There are other instances of misinformation that have developed over the years as the Pacific war recedes further into world history. It is for that reason that this book reviews the facts about the airplane in hope that it will dispel certain myths and underscore salient features. In the years following the Pacific war, documents previously classified about the Zero have become available, and more importantly, those who were responsible for the development and deployment of the Zero have spoken about the airplane more freely, all of which adds greater richness to the aircraft's history.

It is hoped, therefore, that this coverage of the Zero is presented in a balanced form that will give the reader a greater understanding of historical, operational, and technical details that have made this airplane so important in the annals of aviation.

Acknowledgments

Every author relies on the help of many people to complete his or her book.

In this regard, I am indebted to many people, but there are four in particular that made the preparation of this book almost a team effort through endless telephone conversations and letters. James F. Lansdale and James I. Long have been foremost in almost constant consultation on technical aspects of the Zero. They contributed technical details of the various models of the Zero and development of each, and the finer points of corrected production figures that include a breakdown of serial numbers of the Zero, published for the first time. Their counsel and guidance was always there. My special thanks to them both. Osamu Tagaya's involvement became priceless in relating Japanese points of view in many aspects of the Zero fighter, many of which were never published before. He is a true historian of the air operations in the Pacific. Then, there is my ever willing mentor, Shorzoe Abe, who helped with not only the many general aspects of the Zero, but provided much original source material on the development of the engine and armament for the Zero, most of which has not been available to English readers before. To these four dedicated historians, I owe much of the credit for completeness of this book. My sincere thanks!

When writing of Japanese subjects, a Western author must rely heavily upon Japanese friends and contacts that are knowledgeable about the subject. In this regard, my thanks for their assistance go to Saburo Sakai for writing the foreword to this book and relating his operational experience with the Zero. His daughter Michiko Sakai Smart translated the foreword and the continued correspondence after visits with Mr. Sakai. Ichiro and Hisako Naito were very helpful for their contribution to firsthand knowledge about the Zero. Another long-time friend, Toru Miyagi was so very helpful with certain translations, making contacts in Japan for me, and as my companion-interpreter when I visited Japan.

Special thanks to artist and historian Rikyu Watanabe for the use of his outstanding illustrations.

Many have contributed their photographs for this book. Operational photos as seen from the Japanese camera appear here for the first time in a English language publication. For these photographs, my deepest thanks go to Shoichi Tanaka. John and Donna Campbell opened their photo archives to this project, as well. The excellent color contributions of currently flyable Zeros came from photographer Brian M. Silcox, as well as Edward T. Maloney, the latter of the Planes of Fame.

For their many contributions, my thanks go to David Aiken; Harold Andrews; John L. Kelley, MD; Harvey Lippincott; Howard L. Naslund; Harold N. "Nick" Wantiez; Howard M. "Bud" Voss; and the late Albert F. Makiel.

My patient and understanding wife, Ramona, deserves her thanks for sharing otherwise times together.

To all those mentioned, and those in my thoughts who have assisted in this project, I send my deepest thanks and appreciation.

Chapter 1

Ancestry of the Zero

Serious interest in air power in the Imperial Japanese Navy can be traced to the Washington Treaty of 1921. This treaty imposed the so-called 5:5:3 ratio on Japan which restricted its tonnage of battleships and battle cruisers to three-fifths that of the United States and Britain. The treaty applied the same ratio to aircraft carriers, but no restrictions were placed on naval aircraft, although restrictions were occasionally discussed. Thus, when Japan began to search for ways to offset the restrictions on its surface fleet, air power was recognized as the solution.

To begin its new program of building strength through air power, Japan looked to other nations to provide guidance, equipment, and training. During the World War I, Britain had demonstrated an ability to use naval aircraft to support its fleet. It was logical that the Japanese Navy would turn for assistance to the Royal Navy, with whom it had enjoyed long-standing links. Beginning in April 1921, 30 British naval officers arrived in Japan and began actively training JNAF pilots the following September at the newly constructed Kasumigaura airfield and seaplane base north of Tokyo.

Over the next 18 months the British mission introduced the Japanese to the latest techniques in torpedo bombing, navigation, reconnaissance, aerial photography, and other aspects of military airmanship. Perhaps the most significant concept taught to Japanese naval planners was the use of land-based aircraft with sufficient range to support a fleet in combat. Thus, a fleet of limited size need not lose its surface mobility to the shipboard requirements of aircraft while retaining the advantages of aerial support. This doctrine of insisting on acquiring long-range aircraft became a major and important aspect in planning the design of the JNAF's future aircraft. The Zero would become known for this distinct advantage—impressive radius of action.

From this early time of Japanese Naval air power, five generations of fighter aircraft evolved that led to the development of the Zero. This line of fighters and other tactical aircraft began when aircraft carriers came into fleet use by the world's major naval powers in the early 1920s. The Japanese were first to complete and launch a true aircraft carrier, the *Hosho*. Completed in December 1922, the ship was designed and built as a carrier from the keel up; in contrast with the later USS *Langley*, recommissioned in 1925, a conversion from the USS *Jupiter*, a 1913 collier. In 1917, during World War I, the British had converted a battle cruiser into HMS *Furious,* a hybrid carrier with limited flight deck area forward of the superstructure; the battle-cruiser armament was kept aft. The ship was recommissioned as an aircraft carrier in 1925.

This was at a time when Japan was embarking on its own aircraft industry. In so doing, it was heavily influenced by foreign designs and designers. The Mitsubishi Internal Combustion Engine Manufacturing Company, located in Kobe, established a separate division in Nagoya as the Nagoya Aircraft Works in May 1920.

To assist in this new venture of manufacturing aircraft, Mitsubishi employed the services of Herbert Smith, formerly with Sopwith in England, as their chief designer. With a sole-source contract from the Navy to build aircraft, the company developed as their first effort in this field, a series of carrier-borne aircraft for various missions. Because of Smith's influence, this first in a series of new fighters carried the features seen in earlier Sopwith designs. Completed in October 1921, the new model was designated Type 10 Carrier-Based Fighter (signifying that it was accepted in the tenth year of the *Taisho* era). These aircraft have the distinction of being the first fighters designed for carrier operation, while aircraft of other nations at that time were adaptations

of existing land-based fighters. At the onset, the performance of the Type 10 Fighter, powered by the Mitsubishi-built Hispano-Suiza 300hp engine, was comparable to, if not better than that of other fighters operated from aircraft carriers by other nations. Their greatest drawback was that they remained in service far too long.

The second generation of Japanese shipboard fighters, which entered service in 1929, was also influenced by foreign design. This time the Nakajima Airplane Company had won the competition with their license-built Gloster Gambet. This British design, stemming from the Gloster Grebe of 1923 vintage, became the Type 3 Carrier-Based Fighter (Type 3 identified the third year [1928] of the *Showa* era). Unfortunately, this fighter design was already sadly outdated upon delivery. This was at a time when the US Navy was outfitting its three carriers with the far more advanced Boeing F4B-1s, supplementing late-model Curtiss F6C-3 fighters.

The inherent obsolescence of the Type 3 fighter did not deter Japan from using it against the Chinese. . These fighters served until 1935, their later years in second-line roles. For this time period, nearly all carrier-based fighters were equipped with engines of the 400–500hp range, including this Nakajima Type 3 fighter. Although the Type 3 was an outdated design for worldwide front-line carrier fighters, it was the lightest and considered the most maneuverable. In combat against aircraft of other nations, however, it would have lacked speed and firepower.

When Japan adopted a new designation system for its Navy aircraft in 1927, the Type 3

Japan's first aircraft carrier, Hosho, *was completed in 1922, adding new dimension to Japanese naval aviation. Japan excelled in the early use of this and other carriers for extending airpower.*

In 1921, a group of 30 British naval officers were invited to Japan to provide training and demonstrate aerial tactics for the Japanese Naval Air Force (JNAF). The British training program stressed the importance of land-based aircraft with the long-range capability to support fleet operations.

fighter was assigned the earliest designation in this system as A1N1, a system that would prevail through the Pacific war. In this system, the "A" series signifies carrier-based fighter, first in the new designation series, while "N" shows that the design was by Nakajima. This closely resembles the US Navy method of designations used from 1922 to 1963.

As the Japanese aviation industry grew, it became less dependent on foreign designs, yet was not hesitant to use the best forms of technology found in foreign equipment and improve upon it. The third set of Japanese carrier-borne fighters was the Nakajima Type 90. When these came off the production line in 1931, they were modern fighters by world standards. Japan had caught up. Production of

100 of these fighters rapidly replaced the two-year-old A1N1 models which by now were actually outdated by eight years in comparable design technology. The design, although Japanese, was influenced by the Boeing Model 69B, the export version of the F2B, of which Japan had purchased one example in 1928. For JNAF fighters, superior maneuverability was always paramount, and this airplane demonstrated that quality. It was given the short designation A2N1 after it was accepted by the Navy.

The A2N1 entered service in 1932 and remained a front-line carrier fighter for the next three years. Its contemporaries were the US Navy's Boeing F4B-3s and -4s with their more advanced all-metal fuselages, and Great

Britain's Hawker Nimrods, which were navalized versions of the Royal Air Force (RAF) Fury.

France was the fourth country to launch an aircraft carrier in this growing period of naval airpower, the *Bearn*, in 1926. Throughout the ship's operational life, it carried French-built parasol-wing fighters that were adapted from land-based aircraft for carrier use. France capitulated in 1940 before upgrading to more modern aircraft.

Japan held to the biplane design for its fourth generation of carrier-borne fighters, which began in the mid-1930s. This was a refinement of the A2N, Type 90, which became the Nakajima A4N, Type 95 fighter. These cleaner biplanes entered production in 1935. A little faster than the A2N, the A4N was not fully compensated for in speed by the increase in power of the 670hp Hikari engine because of its increased weight. Thus, pilots preferred the agility of the earlier model. This pilot preference would emerge again in the heated dis-

The Mitsubishi Type 10 Carrier-Based Fighter was the first aircraft, worldwide, to be designed primarily for carrier operations. To assist in designing this aircraft, Mitsubishi employed the services of Herbert Smith as their chief designer. Smith's new design was influenced by his earlier work with the Sopwith company in England, so the Type 10 features seen in earlier Sopwith designs. Type 10 referred to the tenth year of Emperor Taisho (1921), the year of type acceptance. John Stroud

Entering service in 1930, the Nakajima Navy Type 3 Carrier-Based Fighter was among the best in the world, in its class. An adaptation of the Gloster Gambet, built under license, the aircraft represented Japan's fighter strength during the Shanghai Incident of 1932.

cussion over the design of the Zero when a choice in performance between speed and range became an issue. Due to the shorter range of the A4N, its activities were limited during the initial stage of the Sino-Japanese Incident. These were the last biplane fighters for the Imperial Japanese Navy.

Enter the Monoplane

It was at this point—the generation of Navy fighters preceding the Zero—that the Japanese not only equaled, but in some standards surpassed other nations in producing carrier-based fighters. The new Mitsubishi Type 96 Carrier-Based Fighter, having the short designation of A5M as a service aircraft, was the first of the low-wing monoplanes for carrier duty, a configuration that all future designs would follow—worldwide. A compromise had been made here, openly objected to by a number of Navy pilots, for improving speed and range at some sacrifice to maneuverability by departing from the biplane arrangement. These monoplanes went into service on September 18, 1937, and were soon operating from the aircraft carrier *Kaga*.

The A5M, later given the code name Claude by the Allies, arrived none too soon for the Japanese as the second Sino-Japanese conflict flared up again. Replacing obsolete A2N and A4N biplanes, they quickly gained mastery of the air. They were a superior opponent to all aircraft types the Chinese could muster. The overall performance of these new all-metal monoplanes seemed ignored by other nations, perhaps not only because of Japan's apparent isolation from the rest of the world, but also because pilots at that time still clung to the biplane concept with emphasis on maneuverability.

Continuing with this philosophy, the US Navy carriers had, as standard equipment, Grumman's stubby F2F and F3F biplanes featuring retractable landing gear. The British Fleet Air Arm replaced their Nimrods in 1937 with Gloster Sea Gladiator fixed-gear bi-planes. The service life of the Gladiator extended into the early war years, until they were replaced by Grumman G-36A aircraft that were originally ordered by the French for their aircraft carrier, the *Bearn*, and later by G-36 Martlets supplied under lend-lease to the British.

The success of Mitsubishi's new monoplane fighter did not come with ease. The company faltered badly in an earlier attempt to use this single-wing configuration. In an effort to meet a 1932 requirement for a 7-*Shi* experimental fighter, little time was granted to Mitsubishi to perfect its design for a new low-wing carrier-based monoplane before being pushed into premature production. Specifications issued by the Navy for the 7-*Shi* fighter left little latitude for designers based on current capabilities. Due to the engineering level of Japan's aviation industry, the undertaking was too advanced and the new test series ended with only two aircraft as an almost total failure.

Nakajima Type 90 (A2N1) Carrier-Based Fighter, a third-generation Japanese naval fighter. Nakajima fighters remained dominant in Japanese naval service until the initial stage of the Sino-Japanese War that began in 1937.

(When a Navy specification was established for a new aircraft, it was assigned a *Shisauku Seizo* number, literally meaning "trial manufacture," and shortened to *Shi*. The number 7, for example, was that of the *Showa* numbered calendar year [1932]. If the aircraft was accepted by the Navy, this designation was replaced with an official service designation consisting of a type number and a mission-descriptive title.)

When the specifications were issued for the airplane that eventually became the A5M fighter, no mention was made of carrier-based equipment. Referred to in its early state as the 9-*Shi* fighter, only five basic requirements were specified: speed, climb, fuel capacity, armament, and maximum wingspan and length. This gave the Mitsubishi design team, led by a young engineer named Jiro Horikoshi, considerable latitude in which to innovate for designing a more suitable aircraft. In this regard, Horikoshi was quoted later as saying: "Since each man, and the group as a whole, had benefited from the knowledge and experience of working on the 7-*Shi* fighter, I was able to incorporate into my new design several novel ideas which represented a marked change over former practices. I could determine without hesitation the general policy, the aircraft's basic configuration, and details of the design, and expect full support from every member of the team." This was a major change in attitude allowed by the *Kaigun Koku Hombu* (Naval Bureau of Aeronautics [BuAir]) in giving such freedom of design concepts to a corporation and design team. It became a major learning process as well for Horikoshi, for it would be this young engineer as chief designer who one day would create the Zero.

In the design concept of the new 9-*Shi* fighter, the thickness of both the wing and the fuselage were kept to a minimum. The landing gear remained fixed, but was streamlined to the greatest extent possible. Its length was shortened through the use of an inverted gull wing. Retractable landing gear was an essential feature on modern aircraft, yet Horikoshi estimated that disadvantages in increased weight and mechanical linkage problems would not justify the speed increase. The fixed gear accounted for 10 percent of the minimum resistance of the entire aircraft; if retracted, it would only have given about 3 percent increase in overall air speed.

Great effort was given to perfecting flush riveting for the exterior skin of the airframe. This was an innovation just being introduced in German and American designs. Every consideration in streamlining was given careful study. When the structure was completed, skin crevices and irregularities were filled and painted to a smooth finish. Although a

A further improvement over the A2N1, this Nakajima Navy Type 95 Carrier-Based Fighter (A4N1), the JNAF's last biplane fighter, was in time for service in the Sino-Japanese War of 1937.

In the mid-1930s, the Japanese Navy was the first in the world to introduce and successfully implement a monoplane design for carrier use. Here is a Mitsubishi Navy Type 96 Carrier-Based Fighter taking off from carrier deck.

218mph (190kt) maximum speed in level flight was called for in the design specification, the 9-*Shi* fighter reached 280mph (243kt) during initial tests. Equipped with an engine that developed only 600hp, its high speed was attributed to its very clean design, rather than an abundance of power. This design philosophy would become a major factor in the success of the Zero.

Every weight-saving measure was taken. Engineers concluded that even 90–110lb saved could effect the ultimate success in an air engagement. Horikoshi said, "The margin of 100lb between two opposing fighters was considered comparable with the difference between a veteran pilot and an unskilled novice. The fighter pilots compared themselves with the old *kendo* [Japanese fencing] champions, and asked for fighters with the quality of the master craftsman's Japanese sword. As a result of our pilot's figurative demand for the blades and arts of the old masters, the Japanese fighter planes were the lightest in weight and amongst the most maneuverable in the world. Our pilots sought tenaciously to master every trick of the superior fighter pilot, and they became well known for their prowess."

The delay between the final approval of the 9-*Shi* airframe and its acceptance as the Type 96 Carrier-Based Fighter (A5M1) stemmed from the lack of a suitable engine. A number of radial engines and one inline engine, varying from 600 to 800hp, were considered by the Navy. Finally, the 600hp Nakajima Kotobuki 2-Kai-1, having the most reliability, was adopted for the initial production models. The gull wing was dropped in favor of a more conventional form to simplify production.

The performance of the early production models was lower than that which was demonstrated by the prototypes, but they went into service anyway in the Sino-Japanese war, which began in July 1937. They became the backbone of the JNAF's fighter force, and over 1,000 were built in several models. The model produced in greatest quantities was the A5M4, which remained in production at Mitsubishi's Nagoya plant until 1940. As powerplants improved, these late models were equipped with the Nakajima Kotobuki 41 and 41-*Kai* engine, rated at 710hp for takeoff.

This airplane, known to the Allies by the nickname Claude, was the fifth generation of Navy carrier-based fighters that preceded the Zero. Although their service at this stage of their operational life became limited, a token number were used in the central and Southwest Pacific during early 1942. Most of these open-cockpit, fixed-landing-gear fighters were retained in Japan by second-line and training units. It was this airplane, however, that designers and the Navy would use as a measure when creating fighter design qualities that would evolve into the Zero Fighter.

The standard fighter of the US Navy in the mid-1930s was this Grumman F3F that outfitted all US carriers. The rest of the world did not take notice of Japan's advanced technology in having already converted to the monoplane design.

With the outbreak of the Sino-Japanese War in 1937, the newly produced Mitsubishi Navy Type 96 Carrier-Based Fighter (A5M) was a welcome replacement for the earlier biplane fighters.

Chapter 2

Meeting the Requirements

To some, it may have seemed premature, but at a time when the A5M Claude was reaching full production and just entering service, the JNAF was already looking for a new airplane as its replacement. Through the Navy's past and sometimes bitter experience, planners had learned that by the time an aircraft completes its development period and enters production, normally a span of three years, the events of quickly advancing aviation technology makes that airplane already obsolete.

For what would become the Zero Fighter and initially called the Navy Experimental 12-*Shi* Carrier-Based Fighter, the *Kaigun Koku Hombu* (BuAir) submitted preliminary planning specifications to the two leading Japanese fighter aircraft companies, Nakajima and Mitsubishi. These specifications were received at Mitsubishi on May 19, 1937, a mere six months after the Navy accepted that company's newest fighter, the A5M Claude, a fighter that would not see combat in China until the following September.

Involved from the onset was their chief design engineer, Jiro Horikoshi. He had joined Mitsubishi at age 23, after graduating from the newly formed Facility of Aeronautics at the Imperial University of Tokyo. Soon after joining the company, Horikoshi was sent to Europe and America to observe aircraft design and manufacturing. Now at age 34, he would shoulder the responsibility for the successor of his earlier A5M Claude, which would become the Zero.

The design specifications for the new fighter, often referred to as the 12-*Shi*, held fantastic demands, however. Not only was this to be an improvement over existing designs, but it was to contain all the qualities of a fighter aircraft in one design, emphasizing maneuverability, range, and endurance. It was customary for a fighter to have *one* of these qualities, but always at the expense of the other two. For one fighter to meet all of these demands would make it—without question—the best fighter in the world.

"How does one improve upon something that is already the best that one can do?" was Horikoshi's wonderment when faced with the new task. As if these initial requirements were not demanding enough, the Navy increased them in October 1937, seemingly beyond reason.

It would be two years before the 12-*Shi* was officially designated the Navy Type Zero Carrier-Based Fighter. From this came the more recognizable name Zero or Zero Fighter. To avoid possible confusion, "Zero" will be used when describing this early time period, whereas "Experimental 12-*Shi* Carrier-Based Fighter" would be more correct.

As mentioned, incorporating the 20 new specifications requested by naval planners meant that the Zero would surpass any existing aircraft or those in the planning stage. The specs were as follows:

Mission: A fighter capable of intercepting and destroying enemy attack bombers, and of serving as an escort fighter with combat performance greater than that of enemy interceptors.

Dimensions: Wingspan less than 39ft 4in (12m).

Speed: Maximum speed exceeding 270kt, 310.5mph (500km/h) at 13,123ft (4,000m) in level flight.

Climb: Climb to 9,843ft (3,000m) within 3min 30sec.

Endurance: Normal flight duration of 1.2–1.5hr with normal rated power (maximum continuous) at 9,843ft (3,000m) fully loaded with auxiliary fuel tank; 1.5–2hr at 9,843ft (3,000m) using normal rated power, or 6–8hr at maximum range cruising speed.

Range: 1,010nm (1,870km) with normal load and 1,685nm (3,110km) with drop tank.

Takeoff: Less than 229.7ft (70m) with head wind of 30mph,12m/sec (43.2km/h) and approximately 574ft (175m) in calm wind. Must be able to take off from a carrier deck.

Landing speed: Less than 58kt, 66.7mph (107km/h).

Gliding descent/min: 690–787ft (210–240m).

Maneuverability: Equal or better than Type 96 Fighter A5M.

Engine: Mitsubishi Zuisei Type 13 (875hp at 11,811ft [3,600m]) or Mitsubishi Kinsei Type 46 (1,070hp at 13,780ft [4,200m]).

Armament: Two Oerlikon Type 99, 20mm machine guns Mk.1, Model 3, and two Type 97, 7.7mm machine guns.

Bombs: Two 66lb (30kg) bombs or two 132lb (60kg) bombs.

Radio: Type 96-ku-1 airborne radio and Type Ku-3 radio homer.

Auxiliary equipment: Oxygen system, engine fire extinguisher, lighting equipment, and standard aircraft and engine instruments.

Structural strength:
Situation A: (final phase of pull-out from dive): Load factor: 7.0; Safety factor: 1.8.
Situation B: (initial phase of pull-out from dive): Load factor: 7.0; Safety factor: 1.8.
Situation C: (limiting speed of dive): Load factor: 2.0; Safety factor: 1.8.
Situation D: (recovery from inverted flight): Load factor: 3.5; Safety factor: 1.8.

(It is interesting to note that these specifications for this Zero were like that of the Claude fighter in that both had omission of maximum weight and size restrictions, including mention of carrier-based operating equipment except for takeoff capability.)

Following receipt of these specifications, Nakajima withdrew from the competition, citing previous commitments in designing and building other aircraft. The real reason appears to have been that Nakajima gave up any hope of being able to meet the stringent Navy specifications. This left only Mitsubishi to satisfy the Navy's most demanding design.

Horikoshi had a most perplexing problem. Here was a fighter requiring a range of more than 1,685nm (3000km), and the previous fighter had a range of 865nm (1,600km). To reach this goal, more fuel would have to be carried, yet the new fighter was to be as maneuverable and have a greater speed than its predecessor. Such combinations were not compatible in a single aircraft design at that time.

Setting all restrictions aside, real or imagined, Horikoshi approached the challenge of designing this "super fighter." Selecting the engine was to be the first major task. By far, the engine is the most critical element in a fighter.

Engine Selection

At this time in 1937, designers realized that there was a grave technical gap in engine availability for the new fighter. The nine-cylinder Hikari of the 710–800hp range had already reached its growth limit and had insufficient power for an advanced fighter. The next possibilities were one of two twin-row radial engines that Mitsubishi had under development. These were the Zuisei 13 of 875hp and the Kinsei 46 of 1,200hp.

Horikoshi rationalized that by selecting the greater of the two, the desired speed and climb capability could be achieved initially rather than having to continually modify the design to achieve the performance demanded by the Navy. But achieving the range called for by the specification was yet another problem. Selecting the larger and heavier Kinsei 46 engine meant that a large and heavy airframe would also emerge. Along with this choice was a demand for a larger fuel capacity with its inherent weight. All of this translated into a greater gross weight for the aircraft, placing upon the airframe the need for stronger and heavier landing gear and structural members. In all, this amounted to an estimated 6,614lb (3,000kg) airplane at takeoff, twice the weight of the current A5M carrier fighter. As a comparison, the estimated weight of the Zero was 400lb less than a normally loaded US Navy F4F at takeoff. Even this weight was considered to be far too heavy, so the Kinsei 46 was dropped from consideration.

Nakajima's Sakae 12 was considered, but because Nakajima was Mitsubishi's competitor, other options seemed better. This left Mitsubishi's Zuisei Type 13 as a choice for a twin-row engine. But it, too, was not fully developed, although the Mitsubishi engine design staff promised that any problems would be resolved by the time the airframe of the new fighter was ready for the engine. The Navy agreed with this solution, and Mitsubishi was delighted that one of their engines would power a fighter of their design. This was contrary to the embarrassing situation with their A5M Claude, which was powered by their competitor's (Nakajima) Kotobuki engine.

Selection of the smaller Zuisei 13 engine resulted in a marked reduction in expected weight. This, Horikoshi calculated, would make the takeoff weight about 5,070lb (2,300kg) and would reverse all the other negative factors of the Kinsei 46 engine concept. With the smaller and lighter weight airframe, an improved range would be gained with a smaller amount of fuel to be carried. From this point of decision making, the design considerations would proceed with the 840hp Zuisei 13 engine. This selection would keep the power loading under 5.5lb/hp, a Navy design requirement.

Such a limiting factor must have been an issue of frustration to this chief designer of the Zero. Here it was that Horikoshi was having to develop a fighter expected to compete with a generation of potential enemy fighters that were already being fitted with engines of over 1,000hp, some of which were envisioned to reach 2,000hp.

The following data show a better comparison of the two engines in question and the Sakae 12 that was eventually used. All three engines are radial, air-cooled 14-cylinders.

Nakajima had persisted with the development of their Sakae 12 engine. Despite their late start when compared to Mitsubishi's twin-row engine projects, the Nakajima engine began showing greater promise, so the Navy decided that the Zero should be powered by

Engine manufacturer	Mitsubishi	Mitsubishi	Nakajima
Engine type	Zuisei 13	Kinsei 46	Sakae 12
Rated hp/takeoff hp	875/870	1,070/1,000	950/940
Rated altitude (m/ft)	3,600/11,800	4,200/13,800	4,200/13,800
Rpm/reduction ratio	2,540/0.728	2,500/0.700	2,500/0.688
Diameter (in)	44.16	47.95	45.28
Dry weight*(lb)	1,158	1,233	1,167
*Without accessories.			

the Sakae 12. Beginning with the third prototype, the Nakajima engine would power the Zero. Not only was greater reliability expected, but there also would be a gain of 75hp with the 950hp Sakae 12 over that of the Zuisei 13.

Airframe Design

The next phase was to determine the general shape of the fighter. Wishing to remain simplistic, Horikoshi selected a very basic configuration. Contrary to earlier Horikoshi de-

Zero Fighter designer Jiro Horikoshi peers into the cockpit of a salvaged Zero in the early 1960s. At that postwar time, only a handful of Zeros survived as testimony to this legendary Navy fighter aircraft.

The appearance of the Mitsubishi Navy Type 96 fighter gave immediate air superiority to the Japanese Navy in their war with China. Tides quickly turn, and a replacement design soon followed—the Zero Fighter.

signs, this fighter was to have a retractable landing gear. He opposed this feature on his previous fighters, recognizing that considerable weight could be saved by making the landing gear fixed and well streamlined. To reach the newly increased demand for speed, however, a retracting gear was now essential regardless of the weight penalty.

An attempt was made to save weight in other parts of the structure. Horikoshi examined all possibilities, including previously established standards. From 1932, all aircraft design work had to adhere to certain structural limitations and requirements. One of these was a load factor of 1.8, regardless of aircraft type. In the case of fighter aircraft, most were designed to withstand a force of 7g, meaning seven times the force of gravity. Because of this, all airplane parts must be able to withstand a load of 12.6g (1.8x7).Considerable weight could be saved by reducing that factor on the less critical parts. It was unreasonable to expect a component designed for 7g flight stress to be able to withstand an additional 5.6g. Horikoshi felt that considerable weight could be saved in this regard, yet retain safety through sound engineering practices.

Another weight-saving measure concerned the wing attachment points that joined the outer wing panels to the fuselage. By making a continuous-spar wing in one piece, these fittings could be eliminated. In doing so, the cockpit area of the fuselage would be an integral part to the wing. In order to not have an unmanageable, one-piece airplane overly large for ground transportation when that became necessary, the fuselage was made to separate just aft of the cockpit. Bolting together the two butt formers of the fore and aft portion of the fuselage resulted in a lighter form of construction, as opposed to separating the outer wing panels from the fuselage at heavy

casting points. To further narrow the fore and aft dimension, the removal of the engine at the firewall reduced the total width to that of the wing cord at its widest point (9ft 2in). Nakajima had already used this method with success in the design of their Army Type 97 Fighter (Ki-27 Nate).

The wing spar of an aircraft is generally the heaviest single member of the structure. To substantially reduce the weight for this fighter, a newly developed aluminum alloy of exceptional strength was used. This was Super Ultra Duralumin, sometimes called Extra Super Duralumin (ESD). Pioneered and developed by the Sumitomo Metals Company, this lightweight structural material was in itself a landmark development in Japanese aviation technology. The alloy was rich in zinc and chrome and was similar to modern-day 7075 aluminum material. Compared to previously used alloys, ESD had 30–40 percent greater tensile strength and 70–80 percent higher yield point. Allied aircraft did not use a similar material until the mid-1940s. (*Note:* ESD was fine for its purpose, but this material was known at the time to develop strain lines when rolled or extruded in its forming process. Because of this, for those Zeros and other aircraft that have survived, severe innergranular corrosion has developed on ESD parts, regardless of the care given to the airplane.)

The new Zero became the first in Japan to be designed from the start with a fully enclosed cockpit. In contrast to the worldwide design practice of a raised structure and turtle deck beginning behind the pilot's headrest, the Zero incorporated an all-around vision, teardrop-shaped canopy for the pilot. This concept was preceded only by the British Westland Whirlwind twin-engine fighter. In time, nearly all first-line fighters throughout the world would have this feature; however, it would become more of a clear bubble-type structure than the many individual pieces used in the Zero, a configuration referred to as the "bird cage" type.

Frequent redesign of the overall structure kept improving its aerodynamics in order to increase its speed and range, as well as im-

prove dogfighting performance. The fuselage was lengthened from the original concept in order to provide a more stable platform for the 20mm guns in the wing. For the wing design, Horikoshi selected the Mitsubishi 118 airfoil. This was a development of the B-9 and the NACA 23012 series airfoils that proved successful when used on the Type 96 Fighter, and now reaffirmed in wind-tunnel tests in a slightly modified form. This airfoil not only had the lift-drag curve equal to that of the well-proven B-9, but also had a center of pressure movement only half that of the earlier wing section.

Another feature of the wing was its decreased incidence at the tips, which helped to ward off stalling. Engineers obtain this feature, known as washout, by building a permanent warp into the wing so that the angle of wing setting (incidence) is different at the root than at the tip. The permanent twist causes the initial angle of incidence, set at the root and expressed in degrees, to decrease toward the tip. The original purpose of washout was to correct for engine torque by applying it to one wing only. But designers found it useful on both tips of highly tapered wings as a way of delaying tip stall and the accompanying loss of aileron control. Horikoshi chose to use washout for its stall-delaying advantage, thus improving dogfighting performance. The amount of twist was so small (from 2deg at the root to -0.5deg at the tip) that it could not be seen simply by looking at the wing, except perhaps from the wing tip in.

For the time being, the design of the aircraft was based upon using the Mitsubishi Zuisei engine, even though its was still in the development stage. Also, the constant-speed propeller development was not proceeding at the expected rate. With these two questionable

To save weight, the Zero's design not only called for a one-piece wing spar, but also made the main section of the fuselage an integral part of this structure. For ground movement when necessary, the aft fuselage (foreground) was detachable from the main section.

areas of parallel development, coupled with the severity of weight reduction, there was uncertainty in Horikoshi's mind that *any* of the prerequisites of speed, maneuverability, and range could be met. To continue Zero development, Horikoshi felt that the Navy must set priorities for meeting these criteria, feeling with certainty and disappointment that all three could not be combined into a single aircraft.

In an effort to resolve these issues, officials of the BuAir, the Yokosuka Naval Air Arsenal, and the *Yokosuka Kokutai* met with Mitsubishi representatives, Horikoshi included, on April 13, 1938. (The *Yokosuka Kokutai* conducted operation evaluation and ongoing development work of new naval aircraft, normally following official acceptance. Preliminary testing of aircraft took place at the Naval Air Arsenal, also at Yokosuka.) The outcome of this gathering had the potential to severely alter the destiny of the entire project. At this point, the 12-*Shi* was a well-established design and was nearing the mock-up stage. The actual flight testing was only a year away.

Horikoshi stated his position concerning the combination of speed, maneuverability, and range in one design. Immediately following Horikoshi's presentation, Lt. Comdr. Minoru Genda stated his views. Genda was the Fighter Group Leader (*Hikotai Cho*) of *Yokosuka Kokutai*, and a highly respected combat leader, test pilot, and tactician. He argued that in a fighter, particularly a carrier-based fighter, the single most important characteristic is the ability of the aircraft to engage successfully in close-in fighting. Having this quality, he stated, the need for heavyweight cannon can be replaced by lighter guns and thus improve the aircraft's maneuverability. To further achieve this quality, a sacrifice of speed and range could also be accepted.

Vehemently opposing this concept was Lt. Comdr. Takeo Shibata, a man with equal qualifications. At this time, he was the senior officer in charge of fighters at the Yokosuka Air Arsenal. His words carried the same authority as those of Genda. Shibata pointed out that JNAF fighters were already superior in dogfighting performance to those of other nations of the world. Unfortunately, the air battles over China where fighter protection was needed to defend the bombers was taking place far beyond the range of Japan's fighters then in existence. Therefore, the next fighter must have not only long range, but high speed as well. Even the slightest edge in speed would provide the margin needed to destroy the enemy. Shibata was convinced that the Japanese fighter pilots could be trained to maintain a clear superiority over enemy fighters, even with aircraft of inferior turning radius. To defend his theory he emphatically pointed out that the maximum speed of an aircraft is strictly limited by its power and the design of the aircraft, a factor over which the pilot has no control. On the other hand, in dogfighting, a pilot's skill can compensate for any lack in maneuverability.

These arguments created much soul searching on the part of those responsible for the success of the new fighter. The conference was split without a decision, since there were no grounds on which to challenge the wisdom of either view and since neither side would relinquish their position. When the meeting was concluded with many ill feelings, nothing had changed in the design demands made by the Navy. Horikoshi was more than discouraged.

To evade the stalemate, the Mitsubishi design team was asked to review the requirements set forth by the 12th *Kokutai* in China, which needed this new fighter, along with discussions just heard, and evaluate the embryonic 12-*Shi* Fighter with these demands in mind.

Although the new fighter was well established in the design phase, it appeared on the brink of extinction if one of these three ele-

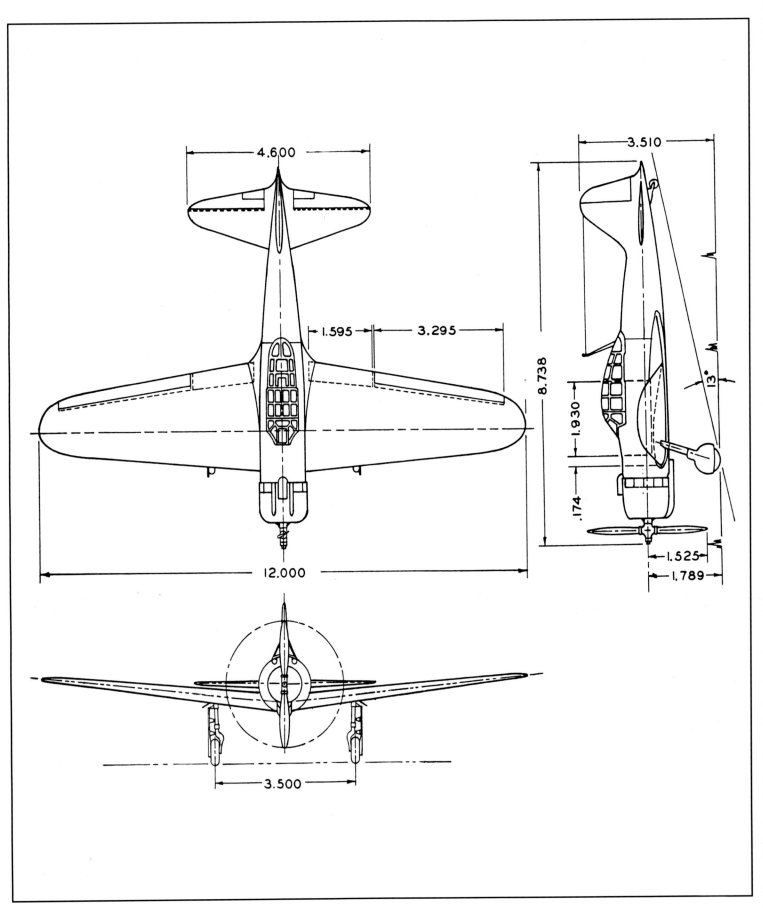

ments was to be enhanced at the expense of the others. This indecisiveness continued for months. Some factions voiced opinions about twin-engine fighters with multiple firing direction armament to handle the demanded escort fighter roll. Others wanted a fast-climbing, high-speed fighter for interception, while still others stuck with the hard and fast rule of dogfighting. To concentrate on any one of these would require a complete new design, now that the problems of meeting all three elements with one aircraft were better understood.

(With regard to the aforementioned twin-engine and interceptor-type fighters, it is interesting to note that a year later (1938) Nakajima was charged by the Navy to develop a 13-*Shi* twin-engine, twin-barrette *escort fighter* with long range, which became the J1N1 Irving. It was Horikoshi, after finishing the design of the 12-*Shi* Zero Fighter, who was tasked to design the J2M1 Jack as a high-speed *interceptor*. Interestingly, the design requirements for both of these fighters were initially met by the Zero.)

Horikoshi compared his earlier computations against the written specifications for the 12-*Shi* Zero, as well as the demands expressed for the new fighter that had been debated. Eventually, he became more convinced that his design could meet all the requirements of speed, maneuverability, and range, if allowed to continue. After presenting his findings to his superiors, the Navy also relented and once again gave full support to the project.

Design decisions for any new aircraft were no simple matter that could be handled on the design floor. Japanese designers were not given the freedom experienced by Western designers. Instead, concepts were passed down from military headquarters, a bureaucracy that was often guided by tradition and outdated policies. New concepts as well as workable ideas were often poorly judged and disregarded as unworkable.

Horikoshi had to work around this stigma if the new fighter was to exceed all prospective enemy fighters. To do this, his design had to be totally independent of foreign technology, even though Japanese airplane designers customarily were a few years behind the more advanced nations, profiting from what they observed from new, foreign concepts.

There also existed a technological gap between Japan and the West. Japan also lagged behind in the development of more powerful aero engines. Japanese aircraft engine development was usually one generation behind that of the Western world. Japanese designers

This is allegedly the No. 2 test-manufactured Zero, known at the time as Experimental 12-Shi Carrier-Based Fighter, A6M1. The first two airframes were powered by the Mitsubishi Zuisei Type 13 engine. Because of vibration problems, a three-blade propeller eventually replaced this two-blade type.

became accustomed to trying to achieve a performance comparable to Western designs while utilizing less powerful engines. This meant having to dispense with all but essential elements of the design and related accessories, while designing to the limit of the aircraft capacity.

The Zero, more than any other airplane, epitomized this philosophy and is the best example of how successful it could be when all conditions were right. This philosophy well reflected Japanese mentality. The present-day affluence of Japan is very much a recent phenomenon. Historically, the Japanese have been inured to a harsh and frugal life on a resource-poor chain of islands, and this naturally reflected itself in the people's attitudes. While such attitudes may be admirable in many ways, in the field of aircraft design it tended to produce machines with very little margin for modification, designs which had little, if any, "stretch" built into them.

In contrast, America was a land of material abundance and wide-open spaces. At the risk of being overly simplistic, it may be fair to

say that, compared to Japanese aero engineers of the time, who had to work with limited resources and often inflexible and narrow-minded dictates from the armed forces, American designers had the luxury of resources and a much freer environment in which to work. This was an important aspect and naturally reflected itself in their work.

The American approach to aircraft design was basically to build as much into an airframe as necessary and achieve the required performance by mating it with a sufficiently powerful engine. American designers could add more armor, armament, or fuel tank protection while being reasonably assured that a yet more powerful engine could be developed to meet their needs. For the Japanese, all too often the attitude was that each additional "excess" feature was a knot off the top speed or a mile off the range. It was not until the midwar years that the Japanese came to calculate the weight of armor and fuel tank protection as an integral, necessary part of the overall design equation. This difference in attitude and outlook ultimately became the difference between victory and defeat.

Three-view drawing shows the Navy 12-Shi Fighter in an early stage of development. Only subtle changes in the Zero design became apparent in the years that followed.

Chapter 3

The Finer Points: Engine and Armament

The BuAir was very dictatorial in such matters as engine selection. As the 12-*Shi* Carrier-Based Fighter project developed, the BuAir's choice, the Mitsubishi Zuisei 13 engine, continued to have problems while the Nakajima Sakae 12 gained speed in development and showed promise as a more suitable engine for the Zero. On May 1, 1939, the BuAir directed that the Sakae would be the engine for production aircraft, while the first two prototypes would continue as planned, to be flown with the Zuisei 13.

The Sakae Engine

Pairing the Sakae engine with the Zero airframe appeared to have solved a number of problems for the design team, yet there were many problems ahead to fully merge the engine and airframe into a well-developed fighter aircraft. The success that the Zero eventually enjoyed was to be shared with the Sakae engine as well. Seldom was there mention that this engine also powered other naval aircraft such as the Nakajima B5N2 Kate, J1N1 Irving, and such Army aircraft as the Nakajima Ki-43 Oscar fighter and Kawasaki Ki-48 Lily bomber. While these airplanes remained prominent throughout the Pacific war, it was the Zero that brought recognition to the Sakae engine as an outstanding aircraft powerplant.

Was the Sakae an extraordinary engine, the major reason for the Zero's success? Considering the Zero's initial performance, one might answer in the affirmative. Certainly much of the aircraft's capability was dependent upon this powerplant. Although the Sakae may not be held in reverence in the annals of the world's greatest engines, it should be nominated as a prominent contender for its

The Nakajima Sakae 21 was the second and most effective engine model to power the Zero. Rikyu Watanabe

contribution to the Zero's success.

When the Sakae 12 was first analyzed by Allied intelligence personnel, it was quickly shrugged off as a near copy of an American design, referred to by some as a cross between the Pratt and Whitney Twin Wasp Jr. R-1535 and the Double Wasp R-1830. After all, some of the components found on the Sakae engine carried the nomenclature of prominent American firms. Japan had secured manufacturing rights on a number of aircraft components. When found by Allied intelligence, they were listed as *copies*, an expression that implied theft.

By considering the Sakae an American design, however, it became possible to speak highly of it, although the aircraft itself consistently drew attention away from the engine in technical discussions. At this time, around 1940, Japanese engines were struggling with power ratings in the low teens, while American engines were approaching 1,800hp range.

When briefly looking at the engine that powered the Zero, one must place powerplants in their proper historical perspective. It was just 15 years before the 1937 specifications of the 12-*Shi* Fighter were issued that the sta-

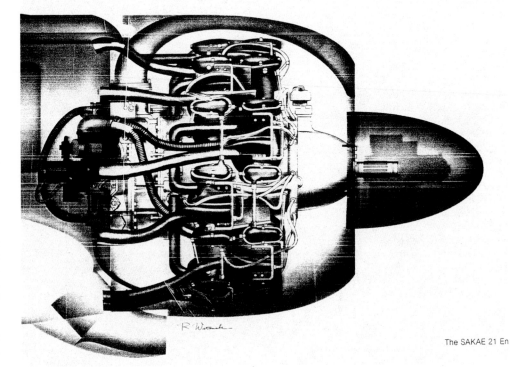

The SAKAE 21 En

tionary air-cooled radial engine came into being. This was construed to be a lighter weight power source than the widely accepted liquid-cooled engines.

The twin-row radial air-cooled engine was the result of a search in the early 1930s for greater engine power without an increase in frontal area. The concept of adding a second row of cylinders in a staggered radial format would increase engine displacement for increase in power without increasing frontal area. In fact, the idea also incorporated decreasing existing frontal area (or diameter) of existing engines by the twin-row concept.

Seemingly, most of the major aircraft engine companies throughout the world began working on this double-row configuration about the same time. Mitsubishi was the first in Japan to consider this line of engine configuration, following the trend set by Pratt and Whitney of the United States. Nakajima, with its practical single-row, nine-cylinder radials—the Kotobuki and Hikari—opted to follow the path of the Wright Aeronautical Company and its Cyclone engine in holding with the single-row concept.

The JNAF felt differently, however, and after convincing Nakajima that they were interested only in twin-row engines for fighters and carrier-based bombers, they awarded Mitsubishi and Nakajima contracts to develop engines of this type. Neither company could lose, for the Navy committed themselves to pay the bills for engine development regardless of the outcome. While 700-800hp was the Navy's goal, both companies' initial efforts in twin-row engines developed closer to 600hp each. However, since further development would be beneficial, the Navy made greater demands on Mitsubishi and Nakajima for their engine power to reach or exceed 1,000hp in the twin-row design concept.

Nakajima's experience in building air-cooled engines began in 1928, first with the British Jupiter 6 which was built under license from Bristol. Nakajima learned further from Pratt and Whitney designs, and by combining concepts used by the two companies, developed their own nine-cylinder radial air-cooled engine by December 11, 1929. This was their very successful Kotobuki engine, referred to as the Nakajima NAH. For years, Nakajima had monopolized Japanese Navy carrier-based fighters with the Kotobuki and the later Hikari engines.

(Nakajima acquired the license from Pratt and Whitney for their Wasp C and Hornet A on December 11, 1929, but by that time, Nakajima had thoroughly analyzed a Wasp already imported and had begun their own design. This became the NAH, later the Kotobuki, early in December 1929, utilizing the best features of the Jupiter and Wasp engines.)

Nakajima's first attempt at a double-row engine was literally putting two Kotobukis together as the NAL. This move enhanced pro-

The Nakajima Sakae 12 was a 14-cylinder air-cooled engine that became the perfect match for the Zero airframe, giving the airplane remarkable performance and reliability. National Archives

ductivity since they already had the major parts in supply. In their second attempt to reach the 1,000hp mark, Nakajima made a number of changes over their first design. The crankshaft was divided, joined at the middle, with a roller bearing in the center for greater support between the two banks of cylinders. In addition, the main connecting rod was of one piece, and pushrods with cams were placed fore and aft of the receptive cylinder banks for better alignment of the intake and exhaust valves. (The Mitsubishi designs retained the pushrods at the front of each cylinder bank.)

With recognized success in this improved version of the NAL engine, it became the 850hp Army Type 97 engine. Production for the Army began immediately not only by Nakajima, but by Mitsubishi as well. With

Army acceptance, their Ha-5 engine was mated to their new bomber, the Mitsubishi Ki-21, Allied code named Sally.

But the Navy insisted on 1,000hp from this twin-row engine. While the NAL design (Ha-5) was still in the process of being groomed for production, Nakajima engineers Takeo Kotani and Masatoshi Tsutsumi began a completely new engine design, void of influence by existing parts. This was the NAM, destined to become the Sakae engine. Improvements immediately realized in this new model consisted of better cooling fin design, improved combustion chambers, and better valve action. Also noted was less vibration, and a more stable combustion pattern. Further enhancement of these features resulted in a NAM II design, which also profited by parallel Japanese advancements in the use of higher octane aviation fuel, better lubricating oils and bearing materials, and higher precision in workmanship and metals finishing. (Throughout the war, Japanese fuel did not exceed a rating of 92 octane.) All of this brought an increase from 2400 to 2700rpm in the NAM II. As a re-

This earliest of the Sakae engines, Model 12s, had a single-stage supercharger. It was considered the most fuel efficient among those that powered the Zero. National Archives

sult, the engine was placed in production in early 1939 as the Navy's NK1B Sakae 11, and NK1C Sakae 12, each having separate optimum operating altitudes.

This rapid success in the early stage of twin-row air-cooled radial engine development brought about the placement of the Sakae 12 engine in the production model Zeros, replacing the intended Mitsubishi Zuisei 13. By this time, the Sakae 12 maximum output was approaching 1,000hp. With this change, Nakajima once again became the engine producer for Navy fighters.

Operationally, the engine was known for its high compression ratio of 7.2 and particularly for its low fuel consumption ratio of less than 190 grams per horsepower per hour at cruise condition. (One source states best fuel consumption to be 160 grams per horsepower per hour.) This allowed the Zero to meet and exceed the specification requirement for long-range cruise, one that surpassed every Navy carrier-based fighter at that time.

Although exceptional in performance, the Sakae was also a temperamental engine in the first year of its service life. It was subject to unexplained vibration problems and high cylinder-head temperatures. This would cause piston seizures and main connecting rod bearing failures, a tremendous work effort on the part of *Kugisho* (acronym for *Kaigun Koku-Gijutsu-Sho*, Naval Air Technical Arsenal) and *Yokosuka Kokutai* during this early part of the test program. While this was an engine development problem, it reflected poorly upon the Zero when it was so essential to place the airplane in operational service.

After the first year of struggling to tame the Sakae, in July 1940 the Navy deemed the engine and airplane, as a unit, sufficiently

groomed for 15 pre-production 12-*Shi* fighters to be sent to Hankow, China. There, with the 12th *Kokutai*, the Zero began its operational service test under combat conditions. With these early planes, a pilot needed considerable skill to properly adjust the throttle and the mixture control to attain maximum range. This skill level requirement was somewhat alleviated with the installment of the AMC (air-mixture control) in late 1940, a device developed by Haruo Niiyama and Shigeto Ueda of Nakajima.

In the service life that followed, advances were made in engine technology that resulted in several series of the Sakae engine. As early as February 1937, efforts began to refine the engine by increasing the takeoff power and high-altitude performance with the addition of a two-stage supercharger. This work, under the guidance of Nakajima's designer Ryoichi Nakagawa became the NAM III. This became the Sakae 21 (Navy code NK1F), which powered the Zero Models 32, 22, 52, 52a, 52b, and 52c. The last in this series was the Sakae 31 which had a water and methanol injection system that was never adequately perfected and generally rendered inoperative on service aircraft. While this model was used in later versions of the Zero, it offered a negligible increase in power.

Armament Package

The purpose of any fighter aircraft is to provide a stable platform for a weapon system that can be placed in the best position to destroy the enemy. As the design of the Zero evolved, these requirements were satisfied with a lightweight airframe to give it the maneuverability and the optimum engine for pursuit. Selecting the best armament was the next consideration.

Throughout the world, there were several combinations of armament being considered during the time the Zero was in the planning stage, around 1938. The Browning .30cal machine gun had been the standard in the United States for a number of years, but the new generation of fighters was being armed with the larger Browning .50cal machine gun. Aircraft cannons were gaining popularity also, but not to the extent of replacing machine guns.

When the Lockheed XP-38 prototype first appeared, its nose contained a cluster of one 23mm Madsen cannon and four .50cal machine guns. Bell's new XP-39 Airacobra used its propeller driveshaft to house the cannon barrel for firing 37mm projectiles, a feature which carried through to the P-63 Kingcobra. Augmenting the one cannon of the Airacobra were two .50cal and two .30cal Browning machine guns.

Already well into production at this time was the Curtiss P-36 with the somewhat archaic firepower of one .30cal and one .50cal Browning machine gun installed in the fuselage to fire through the propeller arc. The P-40 Warhawk that grew out of the P-36 a few years later had four .50cal machine guns to pit against the Zero's two 20mm cannons and two 7.7mm machine guns.

What is even more interesting is the armament package that was first contemplated for what became the Grumman F4F Wildcat, an eventual major adversary to the Zero. In response to a US Navy Bureau of Aeronautics circular of November 1935, this early Grumman biplane design, the XF4F-1, was to be armed with a pair of 20mm cannons. By July 1936, this biplane concept was changed to the monoplane XF4F-2, and first flew 14 months later with two .30cal machine guns over the engine and two .50cals in the wings. Had the original gun concept not changed, the two great Pacific war fighter opponents would have faced each other with identical armament packages. As things turned out, of course this did not come to pass.

The early Wildcat model that first encountered the Zero, the Grumman F4F-3, was equipped with a total of four wing-mounted .50cal guns, and the armament mounted above the engine cowling was deleted. Later versions built soon after the Pearl Harbor attack were increased to six .50cal wing-mounted machine guns.

European trends were fairly consistent, as well. The British had adopted the .303 Browning machine gun for most of its fighters. The Hawker Hurricanes and Supermarine Spitfires that figured so prominently in the Battle of Britain in 1940 were trial fitted with four 20mm cannons in February 1936 and 1939, respectively, but this arrangement was soon abandoned. What became the standard was eight of the smaller 0.303cal weapons so that more in number could be concentrated on the target. Mixed armament was introduced on these airplanes after 1941, and included the 20mm cannon.

The Germans, on the other hand, were relying on heavier weapons rather than quantity. Early production Messerschmitt Bf 109Es mounted four 7.9mm MG 17 machine guns, but later standards called for two MG 17s over the engine and two wing-mounted 20mm cannon.

Changes occurred in weapon systems and combinations as aircraft of all nations advanced to different stages during the war.

Major differences between the Sakae 12 (left) and the Sakae 21 (right) included one- and two-stage superchargers respectively, and engine gearbox housings. An increase of 150 rated horsepower was gained. National Archives

The trends in armament combinations were fairly well established, however. Even JNAF fighter armament followed this pattern. The aircraft that preceded the Zero, the Mitsubishi Navy Type 96 Carrier-Based Fighter, A5M Claude, was armed with two 7.7mm fixed weapons, which were versions of the Vickers machine gun. This weapon proved adequate for air combat over China, but would be inadequate for the new 12-*Shi* Fighter. When developing the Zero Fighter specifications, the Navy felt that world standards would have to be *exceeded* and not merely followed to achieve their goal.

A search had already begun by the Engineering Department of Japan's BuAir to find the most suitable armament for its next generation of fighters. It was the JNAF, not the manufacturer or the aircraft designer, that dictated what armament would be carried on board its aircraft.

In the summer of 1935, serious discussions took place at BuAir regarding standards for machine guns on future naval aircraft. Key participants included Vice Adm. Isoroku Yamamoto, chief of BuAir; Rear Adm. Goro Hara, chief of engineering; and Capt. Misao Wada, chief of staff of engineering. Much of the meeting focused on a report submitted by Japan's Naval Attache in France about the

Oerlikon 20mm cannon, declaring that it showed promise and should be considered. The cannon was still under development in Switzerland; however, in greatest secrecy, Japan soon imported several samples. Japanese weapon specialists liked its highly destructive power with its explosive shell and its light weight and small size. Seemingly, this was a perfect weapon for a fighter.

The following year, 1936, Antoine Gazda, an Oerlikon sales engineer, visited Captain Wada and convinced him that the technical qualities of this weapon were superior. Wada, in turn, persuaded Admirals Hara and Yamamoto that the Navy should acquire the license to manufacture the cannon as its standard weapon. The idea received their unanimous and enthusiastic approval.

Antoine Gazda was not a full-time Oerlikon employee, but a Hungarian Air Force officer who was employed for special projects by Emil Georg Buhrie, the former owner of the Machine Tool Works Oerlikon. Gazda proposed that a rail-transportable factory for the Oerlikon 20mm aircraft cannon be built, one that could be moved easily into tunnels in case of air attacks. The idea was rejected by the Japanese authorities because of its high cost.

At this time, guns as well as telecommunications systems were the responsibility of the

Wartime reports that recorded the Allied evaluation of the Sakae 12 engine gave high praise for the craftsmanship that was evident with these early engines. However, the quality declined as war production accelerated. More than 30,000 Sakae engines were built during World War II.

Kaigun Kansei Hombu, or Naval Bureau of Ships (BuShip). This agency rejected the idea of acquiring the license from Oerlikon and in turn, said that it (BuShip) would be the supplier of "a similar weapon that can easily be developed without foreign assistance."

To obtain the Oerlikon cannon, Admiral Hara concluded that a civilian company would have to acquire the manufacturing license, thus it would be available from indigenous sources. Then the Navy could simply buy it from a Japanese company.

The assistance of *Nihon Tokushuko KK* (Japan Special Steel Company, Ltd.) was thought to hold the solution. They were producers of machine guns, automatic rifles, and 20mm cannon of their own design. Just as negotiations were nearing completion, the Army acquired controlling rights to the company. Three other companies were asked to produce the cannon, but the companies declined. A few retired and influential Navy admirals realized that to produce this cannon, they must form their own company. Secretly, the president of Uraga Dock Company, Ltd., Vice Adm. (Ret.) Takeshi Terashima, agreed in April 1936 to manufacture these cannons under the name of Tomioka Weapon Works of Uraga Dock. It was agreed that the BuAir would purchase all the cannon and munitions shells that this company would produce by a given time, and of specific quantity and quality. Production was to be 60 cannons in 1937 and 100 per year thereafter. By April 1937, however, BuAir changed this to 500 cannons per year. This may well have been because of the Zero Fighter concept being introduced at the time, which included in its specifications two 20mm cannons of this type.

Contract arrangements had been made with Oerlikon of Switzerland, and in March 1938, a group of five engineers led by Kempin and including the son of the Oerlikon development and research chief, arrived in Japan to prepare for production. (*Note:* All were interned by the Japanese when the war began in 1939, not returning to Switzerland until the end of the war in 1945.) Prior to their arrival, production machines and related material from Oerlikon had been sent to Tomioka Weapon Works, which became openly established by the following July. One year later the name was changed to Dai Nihon Heiki KK (Greater Japan Weapon Company, Ltd.). (Other sources state that production was under way by March 1937, and the first Oerlikon-type cannon was completed by the following June.)

In 1935, a Dewoitine D.510 was imported to Japan for evaluation. An impressive feature was the Oerlikon 20mm cannon, a heavy and lethal weapon for that time period. Japan subsequently purchased manufacturing rights.

While preparation for production was under way, *Kugisho* conducted tests on various types of these and other imported cannons such as the Models FF, FFS, AF, and others. In August 1938, a pair of FF cannons were installed on the wing of the Type 95 Carrier-Based Fighter biplane and Type 96 Carrier-Based Fighter (Claude). The intent was to compare these weapons with the FFS-type motor cannon that was mounted in the imported Dewoitine D.510. For accuracy, the FFS proved the best, but the FF cannons currently in production that were mounted in Claude showed the best results in general—except for some horizontal scattering of bullets. Zero designer Jiro Horikoshi was informed of this, but was confident that it could be corrected in his design for the new fighter. This accounts for his placing the tail farther aft for greater recoil stability.

Production of the FF cannon progressed smoothly, but slowly. With Navy acceptance, it became the Type E Machine Gun Model 1 (E for what was pronounced *Oe*, the first Japanese character for Oerlikon). In late 1939, with a change in the official designation system, the cannon became the Type 99 Machine Gun Mk. 1 (or Type 99-1).

According to the Japanese military designation systems, JNAF weapons that were 20mm or *less* were classed as *kikan ju* (machine guns). For the JAAF, weapons that were 20mm or *more* were called *kikan ho* (machine cannons).

The new cannon was now in production, yet the main user, the Zero, was still in the prototype phase. To make the most of these new guns, the Navy decided to divert some as defensive armament on the dorsal blister of the Type 96 Land-Based Attacker, Nell. They were undergoing modification for greater armament, which was found necessary for combat in China. As the Type 99 Flexible Machine Gun Mk.1, these Oerlikons were fitted with a 45-round magazine instead of a 60-round magazine when in a fixed configuration.

Even when the Zero became operational in the skies over China, and Japanese pilots held complete control of the air, this limitation in the number of rounds available to each gun and the low muzzle velocity (600m/sec, or 2,000ft/sec) was a major drawback of the weapon system. Because of this, by May 1940, BuAir had requested *Dai Nihon Heiki KK* to make some corrections. As such, the new model became the FFL cannon with muzzle velocity of 750m/sec (2,500ft/sec), the first prototype of which was completed in September 1941. It was heavier than the earlier model by 10kg (22lb), but was a well-balanced gun. Test firings of the first modified prototype were completed in November 1941, with ex-

Japanese-built 20mm Oerlikon Type 99 Mk. 2 Model 4 Machine Gun

cellent results. As such, it was accepted as the Type 99 Machine Gun Mk. 2.

In addition, BuAir ordered *Dai Nihon Heiki KK* and *Kugisho* in February 1941 to increase the ammunition capacity from 60 to 100 rounds, and to try to achieve a capacity of 120 rounds. Design of the 120 round configuration had to be in the form of an ammunition drum, which was found to be impractical for installation in a thin wing of a fighter. A belt feed system was devised by the spring of 1942, and all tests were concluded in May 1943 for this model, which became the standard.

As demand for the 20mm machine guns increased, *Dai Nihon Heiki KK* established six more factories beginning in 1942, besides the original Tomioka Works. The Navy also had its Toyokawa Arsenal, which was established in 1938, and the Tagajo Arsenal, formed in 1942, manufacture the weapon. By the time the war ended, total production of the Type 99 machine gun reached 35,000 units.

When the initial design of the Zero Fighter was completed, it emerged with two 20mm Oerlikon Type 99 machine guns, one in each wing just outboard of the landing gear. Augmenting the cannons were the tried and proven Type 97 7.7mm machine guns, two of

which were snugly fitted in front of the cockpit above the engine. Each gun had 500 rounds carried in built-in ammo boxes.

Historians rightfully comment on the advanced performance qualities of the Zero when discussing its combat capabilities. Often overlooked is credit for this selection of armament. At that time, however, the quality of the weapons was quickly recognized by Vice Adm. Sadajiro Toyoda, chief of BuAir. On September 14, 1940, Admiral Toyoda prepared a citation recognizing the outstanding performance of the Zero by the 12th *Kokutai*, or air wing, with complete victory over Chungking the day before. This was the first combat encounter by the Zero. Recognition of this outstanding achievement in design was not only sent to *Dai Nihon Heiki KK* for its outstanding cannons, but to Mitsubishi for the airframe, and Nakajima for the Sakae engine. The blend of these three vital elements made the Zero the success that it was on this opening phase of its combat service.

In later years, Zero Ace Saburo Sakai spoke with high praise for this weapon system, particularly the smaller 7.7mm guns in the nose. They were reliable, and seldom jammed. In the early months of combat, most of the victories of the Zero were achieved by these more rapid firing nose-mounted machine guns so necessary in close-in dogfighting.

Chapter 4

The First Flight

No other milestone is more eagerly awaited by those who develop a new aircraft than the day of the first flight. The date cannot always be determined early on in the development program, but as the major details are resolved and fabrication is in progress, that day can be forecast some months ahead. Once set, it is a date that focuses the minds of all those taking part in the creation of a new airplane.

The important strength and vibration tests were finished on one of the three airframes that were being completed. The first of these was to be left merely as a shell for static testing, usually done to destruction. The second airframe (and the first to be counted as an actual flying aircraft) was the more complete prototype that was being readied to meet a scheduled first flight date of March 17, 1939. With justified satisfaction upon first seeing the completed example, Horikoshi described it as "a thing of beauty—having a trim, graceful wing of straight lines and a well-balanced position for its tail. The fuselage was streamlined with few interruptions from the cowling to its aft most tapered point."

Horikoshi was dissatisfied, however, "with the small fin that had been added to improve the spin recovery characteristics." This last-minute alteration was not his idea, and he felt that it disrupted the well-balanced lines that he first envisaged for his new fighter. Horikoshi's book, *Eagles of Mitsubishi: The Story of the Zero Fighter*, does not say what the small fin looked like, but it does mention that it was attached to the underside of the aft fuselage. Some modern drawings of the prototype show such a projection, but often in dashed lines because no photographs or authoritative drawings from the period have come to light to show conclusively the characteristics of this small ventral fin. A surviving photo of the wind-tunnel model suggests that the vertical area was increased by adding some wood at the trailing edge of the rudder and tail cone.

Surviving technical sketches show that both the fin and the rudder were progressively enlarged by extensions fore and aft, bringing into question whether these alterations were steps in the original development, or Horikoshi's attempts to improve the tail after the Navy said the ventral fins would be needed on the first and second prototypes, pending relocation of the tail on the third and succeeding aircraft.

The designer could not help but reflect upon the one long year spent in designing the airplane that stood before him, and which originated from many two-dimensional drawings. In his eyes, it was now a beautiful three-dimensional object. Horikoshi admitted to feeling deep emotions for this creation, something only a designer such as he could understand.

The time came to move the finished airplane to the flying field for the true test of its flying ability. Unlike American and European aircraft manufacturing companies, which normally were located adjacent to an airfield, Japan did not have such a luxury of open space. Only two of slightly more than a handful of Japanese aircraft companies were so fortunate. The reason was that most of the major Japanese aircraft companies evolved within heavy industry plants that originally only needed waterways or railroads for transportation. In the case of the Zero, the Nagoya Aircraft Factory of Mitsubishi was situated at Oye-cho, Minatoku, in the southern congested industrial heart of Nagoya. There was a small airstrip alongside it, but it was suitable only for fly-away delivery of lightweight production aircraft. This modern, high-performance Zero would have to be moved to a suitable airfield for its first flight testing, about 30 miles north, where Mitsubishi had a field facility at Kagamigahara airfield.

To move the Zero to Kagamigahara, its major components had to be separated and packed in large shipping crates. The crates were placed on two ox-driven wagons for the laborious trip. The entourage departed the factory a little past seven o'clock in the evening on March 23, and began weaving its way through Nagoya, Komaki, and Inuyama, over unpaved roads leading to the airfield. The road was graveled in some parts, often resembling paths full of dips and turns. The journey lasted all night and well into the next day. What an archaic way to move the most advanced fighter aircraft in the world!

Trucks could have been used for the move, but the thought was that because of the poor road conditions, a heavy jolt of the faster moving truck could damage the aircraft. Once the airfield was reached, the carts and their contents were moved inside the Mitsubishi hangar where the uncrating and assembly began.

The day of the first flight arrived, April 1, 1939. As the day began, the field was busy with Army flight training, and as usual, this continued until four o'clock in the afternoon. The Mitsubishi enclave waited for the appointed time when the field would be turned over to them for the test flight. When that time arrived, the ground crew rolled the gray semigloss airplane from the hangar to the grass outside. Its black engine cowling was a stark contrast to the rest of the airplane. The fighter seemed to dazzle in the sun that was still bright in the cloudless sky. A fresh wind remained steady from the west, about 7mph.

The pilot to fly this new airplane was Katsuzo Shima, one of Mitsubishi's most experienced and respected test pilots. He was an ex-Navy petty officer, third class, who after his discharge had joined Mitsubishi and had tested many aircraft. Shima was Horikoshi's choice.

The last-minute checks were made by Mitsubishi technicians as Shima reviewed his notes and checked over his equipment. The

Dr. John Kelley at the controls of the Confederate Air Force's Zero, one of the few flyable Zeros in the United States. This aircraft is an A6M2 restored and re-engined with a 1,200hp R-1830 and modified DC-3 cowling. It is shown here in early wartime colors. Brian M. Silcox

engine specialist started the engine and reviewed every detail to his satisfaction. When all was in readiness, Shima settled into the cockpit and adjusted his straps. With a wave of his hand, the chocks were pulled from the wheels, and the airplane rolled away from the group of on-lookers.

The first item on Shima's agenda was to test the fighter's ground-handling qualities. After a series of turns, accelerations, and rapid stops, the wheel brakes were not to his liking. He returned to the starting point, and technicians climbed on the wing to hear Shima's complaints. They quickly made adjustments to the wheel brakes, hoping to have solved the problem, and the airplane moved away for an-

other try. Shima seemed more satisfied this time, so taxied to the east end of the field in preparation for the takeoff.

Everyone watched breathlessly as the sound of the engine came to full life. The airplane responded to this burst of power and it picked up speed, with a trace of dust coming from its wheels. After a brief roll along the sod strip, it became airborne, and climbed to about 30ft as it passed in front of the spectators. At that point, the power was retarded and the glistening fighter settled to the ground. The long-awaited moment of first flight had passed. Shima taxied back to the waiting on-lookers who were eager to hear his evaluation of the airplane.

Once the Zero was parked and the engine turned off, Shima eased out of the aircraft and onto the ground. All those present gathered around him to hear him say that the flight controls responded very well, with his only complaint being the wheel brakes. (Poor braking action would be a problem for the Zero throughout its operational life.) The braking

problem was treated as the least of everyone's worries, and signs of relief were evident. The fighter had flown.

This was but the beginning of many test flights. In the 12 days that followed, Shima and his assistant test pilot for the project, Harumi Aratani, flew six low-speed familiarization flights, all with the gear extended. Both pilots made the observation that flight control response was much like that of the Type 96 Fighter, as intended, but there was undue vibration in all flight modes. After considering many factors and possibilities, it was thought that the propeller might be the cause. It was replaced by a three-bladed propeller, which would change the resonance between that of the engine, the airframe, and the propeller itself. In making this change, the vibration dropped remarkably, and eventually, the three-bladed configuration of the constant-speed propeller became standard for the Zero.

As flight testing moved to a more advanced stage, Horikoshi directed considerable concern toward elevator response. As already

While still known as the 12-Shi Carrier-Based Fighter, this prototype buzzes onlookers at Kagamihara Air Base in 1939 on one of its many test flights. Except for engine type change, the basic design remained fairly constant. Shoichi Tanaka

reported, flight control for the fighter was felt to be quite acceptable, but at high air speeds the elevator was overly sensitive. One solution previously tried was for the pilot to manually adjust the degree of movement by a variable leverage control linkage relative to the air speed. In combat, however, the air speed is constantly changing, and a pilot does not have time to continually make this type of adjustment. Another possible solution was to reduce the size of the elevator so as to not overcontrol while at high maneuvering speeds. This resulted in insufficient elevator for providing adequate control in the landing phase.

Horikoshi had anticipated this problem for nearly a year during the design phase of the airplane. At this point, however, the idea of inducing elastic action into the cable control system came to mind. Already there were set standards for construction materials that

would prevent this from happening in control movement response. If these standards were set aside, the problem might be solved by using finer strands of connecting cables and more flexible torque tubes to the elevator. In this way, at high elevator loads, the cable stretch would cause less movement of the elevators and therefore less control response from the control stick at high speeds. At lower speeds and less pressure, such as in the landing phase, full elevator travel could be expected. Much thought was given to this idea by Horikoshi and other members of his design team. Sensing that it would work, it was installed and tried in the test aircraft. It solved the problem.

The fear of having spongy, nonresponsive control movement due to elasticity of the system did not happen. Obviously, a perfect match was achieved between elasticity of the cables and torque tubes, and the strength needed for maximum control deflection force. To some people versed in flight control, there was a one in a hundred chance that this would not cause control surface flutter at high speed, but with luck or pure genius, Horikoshi obtained the perfect combination. Horikoshi

knew that there would be a time in the future when pilots in other countries would desire the same control characteristics; perhaps they would be surprised to know that the problem had been solved in Japan prior to the outbreak of the Pacific war. Both the variable leverage linkage and the stretchable linkage concepts as applied to aircraft were patented in 1940 in Japan.

On May 1, 1939, a mere month following the Zero's initial flight, Horikoshi was notified by BuAir that beginning with the third airframe, the Mitsubishi Zuisei 13 engine would be replaced with the Nakajima Sakae 12. Now, with this change and a slightly modified tail, the design was stabilized for production as the A6M2. The preceding two experimental aircraft carried the designation A6M1.

Flight testing at Kagamigahara proceeded smoothly and according to an established plan. The four pilots that tested the aircraft were certain that Japan now had the world's most maneuverable modern fighter.

The comparison was specifically leveled at the Heinkel He 112, the Seversky P-35, and the Chance Vought V-145, all of which these pilots had tested in Japan, and which had a maxi-

Flight tests of the prototype Zero continued by Mitsubishi from April 1 to September 14, 1939. On that date, the first Zero was turned over to the Navy at Oppama Air Base in Yokosuka. Other tests continued, honing the Zero to a lethal and nimble fighting machine.

mum speed equal to or surpassing that of the earlier Type 96 Fighter, Claude. To their knowledge, foreign designers had given little attention to the balance between control response and control pressures that Horikoshi was so mindful of. They felt that this aspect could result in an inadvertent spin during tight maneuvers such as encountered during close combat.

In Mitsubishi's concluding report on their new fighter just prior to delivery to the Navy, they made the following comments about the airplane at that stage of its development:

1. A total of 119 flights had been made, accumulating 43hr and 26min. When including engine run time for various ground testing, 70hr and 49min of engine time had been accumulated.

2. At this point, all control demands were met with the single exception of poor response to aileron control at low speed. (Aileron control was a weak area within varying speed ranges for this fighter throughout its entire life, even though modifications would be made.)

3. Flight performance tests were nearly complete with the exception of endurance and rate-of-climb tabulations. The maximum level speed, takeoff, landing, and rate of descent conformed to the original predictions. Maximum speed, even though meeting the specifications for the design, were thought too low for meeting the intended mission for the aircraft, and could only be corrected with a larger engine.

Having completed this phase of flight testing, the A6M1 was fully accepted by the Navy and on September 14, 1939, departed Kagamigahara for Oppama Air Base at Yokosuka to the south of Tokyo. Slightly less than two years had elapsed since Mitsubishi received the original design specifications for the airplane. It had been only four and a half months since the airplane first took to the air. This was considered rapid development for an aircraft of this type and time period.

The second prototype 12-*Shi* carrier fighter incorporated the modifications made on the original test aircraft during its flight test program. On October 18, 1939, the second prototype A6M1 concluded its flight testing. A week later, it was accepted by the Navy and flown away.

Later that month, the first cannon-firing tests were conducted on the second aircraft to examine its capability as a fighter. On the first pass, the aircraft scored nine hits out of 20 rounds fired upon a roughly 13ft by 16ft (19sq-m) ground target. The cannon became basic armament on this and all fighter models that followed.

Production of the Zero began at a slow pace in 1940, reaching nearly 100 by the end of the year. One Zero per day was seen in 1941 at the Mitsubishi plant, whereupon Nakajima was issued supplemental production orders for the Zero beginning in 1942. This company became the largest producer of the Zero, while Mitsubishi remained the engineering developer in conjunction with their production of the airplane. In the years following, the 21st Naval Air Depot and the Hitachi Aircraft Company produced Zeros as well. (See the appendices.)

Chapter 5

Two Zeros Down

With every newly designed and delivered aircraft, there is an air of invincibility stemming from high hopes that this is the ultimate aircraft. When the first of its type becomes involved in a serious accident, regardless of loss of life, this incident is perhaps the most difficult to accept. In the case of the Zero, there were two such incidents with loss of life that became traumatic chapters in the development of the airplane.

Before the first accident occurred, word of this new fighter came to the officers of the fighter units operating in China. These men were experiencing problems with their existing fighters, which were in need of a replacement. The problem was that their A5M Claudes did not have the range to escort the bomber formations all the way to the target areas. Learning of the expected range of the new A6M1, the men sent word that the airplane was needed immediately in the combat area. Horikoshi could not help but have an overwhelming feeling of satisfaction when the front-line units called for *range*, and not a word about *maneuverability*, two issues that had been points of heated discussion.

But the new airplane was not ready for operational service. Much testing was yet to be done, particularly with the constant-speed propeller. The newly devised unit was sluggish in changing pitch angle in relation to the changing air speed, as one would encounter in combat. Sudden acceleration often caused over-speed of the propeller and engine, which is a dangerous situation and could be destructive to the engine.

During one of many flight tests of the second A6M1, on March 11, 1940, Masumi Okuyama, an experienced pilot, was flying overhead at Oppama Air Base. Oppama was adjacent to the Yokosuka Naval Base, home for the Yokosuka *Kokutai*, the main JNAF test and evaluation center for its aircraft, much like that of Wright Field for the US Army during

World War II. Other pilots were on hand on the ground to witness these evaluations, in the event of an accident.

In the first of a series of planned maneuvers for analyzing propeller response to air speed changes, Okuyama started his first dive from nearly 5,000ft. After recovering at 1,600ft, he climbed again for a second dive. At a dive angle of about 50deg, the witnesses on the ground heard the shrill whine caused by an over-speed of the engine, only to be interrupted by a loud explosion, followed by the disintegration of the airplane. Pilot Okuyama was seen to separate from the airplane, his chute blossom, only for him to fall clear from the harness 1,000ft above the water. Some speculated that Okuyama died from the explosion, and that the parachute opened on its own. Others felt that in a semiconscious state, thinking he was about to enter the water, Okuyama disconnected his harness and fell to his death.

Like most accidents in a test program of that time period, before sophisticated test analysis equipment came into play, the cause of an accident left much to conjecture. Again, some speculated that engine over-speed caused severe vibrations that shook the engine from its mounts, and thus caused the airframe to further disintegrate. In support of this theory, the throttle was found in the fully retard position. Also, the elevator mass-balance arm was broken and the counterbalance weight was missing. The arm *could* have broken off on previous flights as a result of landing stress and other factors. With this weight detached, the elevators could be free to flutter, a condition that would become apparent only at increased speeds and would be amplified throughout the entire structure as it persisted. This situation also could occur suddenly, and would explain the separation of the engine since that was a weak structural point, one not designed for the flutter phenomenon.

Few investigators were completely satisfied with this latter conclusion, yet it became the official explanation. Contributing factors could have been an over-speed of the engine, a situation that was later rectified by a more responsive pitch control mechanism for the propeller. Main spar failure due to poor machining was also a factor considered. This was later ruled out through tests made at the Navy laboratory; however, some reservations remained since a time limit of 50 operational flying hours were imposed upon the first 21 airframes. Machining changes were made on all spars that were manufactured following the accident. A more acceptable fix, though, was to strengthen the support arm for the elevator counterbalance on subsequent airframes. No further accidents of this type occurred.

It was 13 months before a second accident with an A6M2 occurred. The second incident began to unfold on the afternoon of April 16, 1941. Sub-Lt. Yasushi Nikaido, from the aircraft carrier *Kaga*, had been performing aerobatics with A6M2 No. 140 (s/n 1140) over Kisarazu Air Base across the bay from Tokyo. After a period of performing loops and tight turns in this A6M2, all of which induced heavy G-loads upon the airframe, he noted skin distortion on both wings. In an effort to determine what aspect of flight loads produced this skin buckling, Nikaido began a 50-degree dive at 290kt with the engine at idle starting from about 12,000ft. As the dive continued, and reaching 320kt, Nikaido began losing control, and started his pull-out. At this point, he felt a severe shock as the aircraft pitched up from the dive, nearly causing him to black out from the force.

Regaining his senses and some control over the aircraft, Nikaido was aware immediately that both ailerons had left the aircraft, and some of the skin from the upper surface of the wing was gone. The pitot tube had been shaken off, freezing the air speed indicator at

160kt. Finding himself near Kisarazu Naval Air Base at the time, the veteran pilot eased his Zero in for a safe emergency landing without further incident. The details of the mishap were reported immediately to BuAir, *Kaigun Koku-Gijutsu-Sho* (Naval Air Technical Arsenal) and *Yokosuka Kaigun Kokutai* (Yokosuka Naval Air Group).

Initially, the incident seemed to point to the recent modification made to ailerons of A6M2 aircraft to try to correct the poor aileron response at high speed. Beginning in February 1941, with A6M2 No. 127 (s/n 3127), each aileron was built with a servo-type balancing tab that helped the pilot overcome heavy roll forces. Immediate speculation was that this new device was allowing the aileron to exert too much pressure on the wing structure.

As part of an investigation, A6M2 No. 135 (s/n 1135), which had been built at the same time as No. 140 and also had the balancing tab, was examined. It was hoped that an in-spection and flight test would reveal the cause of the structural problem. No. 135 had arrived recently at Oppama from the aircraft carrier *Akagi*, along with a report that the aircraft had had in-flight skin wrinkling problems.

In hopes of isolating the problem, Lt. Manbei Shimokawa of the *Yokosuka Kokutai* selected A6M2 No. 50 (s/n 350) for a functional test flight because it had been built in October 1940 and did not have the balancing tabs. Shimokawa was an experienced fighter-squadron leader and instructor pilot at the *Yokosuka Kokutai,* placing him in the most important test and development position within the JNAF. He had been influential throughout the Zero's early development phase, having been appointed to that post in November 1939.

The morning of April 17, 1941, the day following the accident, Shimokawa was airborne and soon established the unmodified aircraft in a 50deg dive from 12,500ft. He began his pull-out at 320kt and leveled at 4,000ft. There was no unusual behavior of the aircraft other than the signs of skin wrinkling, which was typical for a high-G pull-out such as he had just executed.

Having noted these characteristics, next Shimokawa flew the previously inspected No. 135 from the *Akagi*. He expected to duplicate the flight he had just completed in No. 50 without incident. Initiating his dive at 13,000ft and 50deg, he began the pull-out at around 6,500ft. Apparently nothing appeared improper, for Shimokawa climbed to altitude again, this time making his dive at approximately 60deg. At a point during the second dive, ground observers saw parts fly off the plane. The struggling fighter rolled twice to the left and appeared to right itself momentarily, but then the nose suddenly dipped and continued headlong into the sea at 1,000ft off the shore from Natsujima. Lieutenant Shimokawa was killed in the crash.

Japanese Navy Type Zero Carrier-Based Fighter Model 52 owned by the Japanese Air Self Defense Force. It is shown here at Johnson Air Base (now Iruma Air Base), Japan, in 1963, soon after its ini-tial restoration. This A6M5 of the 343rd Kokutai crash-landed on Guam following action with F6Fs during the Battle of Philippine Sea, June 1944.

These are the crash remains of the second Zero accident, caused by structural failure. It was in this A6M2 (s/n 1136) that Lt. Manbei Shimokawa of the Yokosuka Kokutai was killed while investigating structural distortion at high speed.

This unfortunate accident and the loss of a second life in the ongoing development program of this new fighter was one of grave concern. Such incidents make lasting impressions upon each person involved with any new airplane that is experiencing teething problems. Too much was at stake if solutions were not fully resolved, and done so immediately. All possibilities were investigated in a long and methodical process.

Investigating officials concluded that structural failure had been a result of a pre-existing wing flutter problem. This problem was enlarged on airplanes equipped with the balancing tab, for the flutter now began at a lower air speed, making matters worse. Until corrections could be made, all A6M2s with

balancing tabs were temporarily redlined at only 250kt and a limit was placed on dive pull-out stress loads of 5g.

It became apparent that the balancing tab modification had not been calculated into the overall design of the aircraft. It was an initiative that came from the Navy, not the Mitsubishi design team. It had been an afterthought and extraneous to the integrity of the original design conceived by Horikoshi and his staff.

To correct the flutter problem and raise the speed at which it might first occur, Mitsubishi made the following changes on production aircraft beginning in May 1941:
• Increased the thickness of the outer wing skin.
• Installed longitudinal stringers to increase torsional strength.
• Added external balance weights to the ailerons, pending modification of the internal weight configuration.

These measures would have allowed the retention of the balancing-tab system, but Mit-

subishi was forced to remove the device from production-line aircraft shortly after the accident because pilot confidence in the tabs had been utterly destroyed by Shimokawa's crash. As a result, fewer than 80 A6M2s had the balancing tabs, and the device did not appear again on Mitsubishi-built Zeros until the 1943 introduction of the long-wing A6M3, Model 22, which needed the help of the tabs to reduce stick forces. By then, pilot objection to the device had eroded, and they were calling for more maneuverability at nearly any price. The successful reintroduction of the tab device on the Mitsubishi-built Model 22 permitted Nakajima to begin installing the balancing tabs on their version of the Zero Model 21 during early 1943, thus improving its maneuverability as well.

The few Mitsubishi-built A6M2s that had already been produced from February to May 1941 with balancing tabs had the external weights added to their ailerons as a retrofit item, as did every other early Zero still in the Navy's inventory. But the other structural changes were not made to any of them.

The A6M2s produced from May 1941 to mid-September of the same year had all of the improvements listed, and were considered combat-ready aircraft without special restrictions. In mid-September, beginning with A6M2 No. 327 (s/n 3327), Mitsubishi assembly workers began installing a new aileron that had all of the balancing weights inside its nose section, thus eliminating the external weights and any drag induced by them. The A6M2s that went aboard the carriers for the Pearl Harbor attack were, in the main, those produced between May and November 1941. Some had the externally balanced ailerons, and some had the new ailerons with the revised internal counterbalance weights. These planes all had the regulation dive speed limit of 340kt, but the slower rate of roll and the heavy aileron forces were back.

Few English-language writings on the Zero have mentioned the wing-aileron flutter crisis and the impact the situation might have had if Japan had gone to war before the problem was discovered. Shimokawa's death in the faulty Zero had occurred a mere eight months prior to the Japanese attack on Pearl Harbor. Fortunately for the Japanese Navy, within that time, the problem was analyzed and solved, and the newest and best Zeros were in position for placement aboard the attack-force carriers by November 16, 1941. Two days later, these carriers left their home ports to make up the Hawaiian Task Force.

Shortly after the time that the carrier task force left the Kurils on November 26, en route to Hawaii, the speed restriction was raised to 360kt. The matter is not clear, but it seems apparent that the speed restrictions were never lifted from the planes with tabs and external mass balance retrofitted. The Navy probably withdrew them from first-line units and relegated them to second-line service in training units during the second half of 1941.

Shimokawa's accident also affected the future design of all Japanese aircraft, for the technical data generated during the investigation was shared with other Japanese aircraft companies, and with the JAAF as well. The formulas in general use by these agencies, to calculate the point at which flutter might occur, were revised. The loss of Shimokawa was felt keenly by all who knew him, but his death was not in vain.

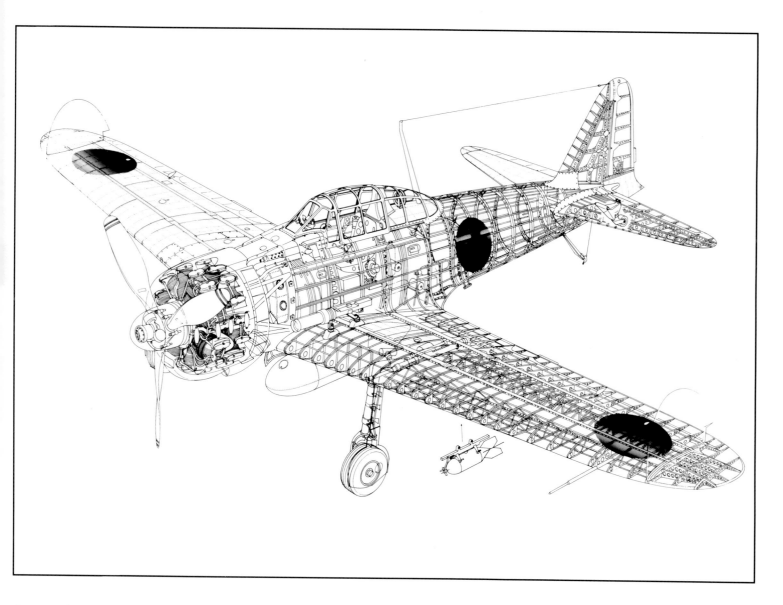

Cutaway of Navy Type Zero Model 21 (A6M2).
Rikyu Watanabe

Chapter 6

Tactical Evaluation

The qualities of the Zero became known to the Navy pilots fighting over mainland China, and they were insistent upon receiving these much needed new airplanes at the earliest possible time. However, Mitsubishi engineers were reluctant to clear the fighters for combat before they had been fully tested. The opinion of Navy engineers differed: the Zero was so promising, they believed any changes could be handled in the combat zone. To support this decision, technicians and engineers were sent along with the Zeros to make whatever modifications were found necessary while in the battle zone.

On July 15, 1940, the first of two sections consisting of six service test models of the Zero from the *Yokosuka Kokutai* departed Japan from Omura Air Base, Kyushu, on their final leg to mainland China. (*Note:* Some sources record the date as July 21, but more reliable sources show this to be incorrect.) Their destination was Hankow, where they joined the 12th *Kokutai* already established there. Each of the two fighter elements was led by a G3M Land-Based Attacker (Nell) which acted as lead-ship for navigation on this long overwater flight. In charge of their respective elements were Lt. Tamotsu Yokoyama and Lt. Saburo Shindo, both of whom became prominent figures in the Japanese Navy later in the war. Upon reaching Hankow, they were joyfully welcomed by the pilots of the fixed-gear A5M4 Claudes. The A5M4 lacked the long-range capability for bomber escort, a feature that was promised on the 24 newly arriving Zeros.

Training flights and ground crew familiarization with the new fighter lasted for one month following their arrival. For those who had been flying aircraft such as the A5M4 fighter, transitioning to the zero, required about two weeks for well-seasoned pilots, while training for the more junior aviators lasted about one month.

With the new fighter now committed to combat use, back in Japan, the Zero was officially accepted by the Navy. In so doing, it was named the Type Zero Carrier-Based Fighter Model 11, and now properly referred to as the Zero Fighter *(Reisen)* as opposed to the 12-*Shi* Fighter. This new designation became effective on July 24, 1940. Its short title was A6M2.

With training completed, a formation of 12 Zeros roared into the air from Hankow on August 19, 1940. Following a refueling stop at I-ch'ung, they joined with Navy bombers for their first combat escort mission. In the lead aircraft was Lt. Tamotsu Yokoyama. Their mission was to escort 54 Mitsubishi G3M Nell

A flight of two A6M2 Model 11s head inland toward targets in China on May 26, 1941. These Zeros of the 12th Kokutai *were flown by Lt. Minoru Suzuki in the lead aircraft, followed by his wingman, PO3c Kunimori Nakakariya. Shoichi Tanaka*

An often-seen photograph of an A6M2 Model 11 along the north bank of the Yangtze River near Hankow, China. The Zero was assigned to the 12th Kokutai, which was one of two units to introduce the Zero in combat. Shoichi Tanaka

bombers to Chungking, a distance of about 390 miles. On previous escort missions, these bombers were accompanied by the earlier A5M4 Claudes to the extent of their range. Once they had to leave the bomber formation for lack of fuel, the bombers were left to defend themselves against waiting Chinese fighters. Aggressive Chinese interceptions during the past six months had begun to hurt the Japanese; their losses were rising. The new Zero arrived on the scene none too soon, for the vulnerable bombers needed protection all the way to the target and back, and the Zero had been designed to do just that—and more.

But where was the Chinese opposition that had been so plentiful on previous missions? The Zero pilots could hardly wait to engage the enemy, for they knew they had the

Well above the clouds while returning from a mission to Hankow, China, in August or September 1941 is this A6M2 of the 12th Kokutai. The pilot seen here is the later-to-be-famous fighter ace Saburo Sakai who loaned his Leica camera to a fellow pilot for this mission. Shoichi Tanaka

These Navy Type 96 bombers required escort fighter protection on their deep, penetrating bombing missions into China. The Zero was able to provide that protection. Note the 20mm Oerlikon cannon in the modified upper blister, one of the first uses of the weapon that was acquired for the Zero.

superior machine. But the Chinese, noted for their intelligence-gathering ability, apparently could foresee the Zero's deadly capability, and knew when that first mission was taking place. There was no contest in the air that day.

On the day following, the situation was the same. Formation leader Lt. Saburo Shindo hoped he would have the chance to engage the enemy for the first time with the Zero. With disappointment, he and his wingmates returned to Hankow without firing a shot.

The Zeros were airborne again on September 12, to escort 27 bombers over Chungking and back. The Japanese pilots were determined to fire their guns at the enemy, even if they had to leave the bombers to do it. As the bomber force left the target area, the Zero pilots spotted what appeared to be five enemy aircraft on the ground, and dove to attack. The enemy aircraft proved to be decoys, but the Zeros strafed the Shihmachow airfield, along with other ground installations. Their actions challenged the Chinese to come up and fight, but none rose to the challenge.

On the fourth mission flown by the Zeros on September 13, the situation changed. It became their day of "first blood," creating a legend that would build throughout World War II, and be remembered well beyond then. Once again, the Zeros were escorting the

bomber force deep into mainland China for another attack on Chungking. As before, not one Chinese fighter rose to the attack, and the Japanese bombs rained on the city.

This time, however, the Japanese would *make* things happen. Like the day before, the attacking force of 13 Zeros left the target area, leaving a C5M Babs (Mitsubishi Type 98) reconnaissance aircraft once again to loiter in the target area. During that loitering period on September 12, the post-strike reconnaissance Babs had noted that shortly after departure of the strike force, 32 Chinese fighters appeared over the city and flew a show-of-force demonstration for about 20min, then landed at the airfield. Twenty-minutes after landing, the planes took off again and disappeared to the northwest in the direction of Chengtu.

Clearly, the Chinese fighters were demonstrating their defense capability for the benefit of the civilian population, while carefully avoiding actual combat with the new Japanese fighters. The Japanese then executed their strategy by departing the target area together with the bombers, withdrawing to a point about 40mi east of Chungking. When the Babs crew reported the return of the Chinese fighters to the target area, the Zeros turned around and headed back to Chungking. Their hopes were high that this time they would catch the Chinese fighters as they once again were demonstrating for the civilians.

The Japanese strategy worked perfectly. Wheeling around toward the city and climbing for an advantage in altitude, Lieutenant Shindo led his flight of Zeros in a classic situation of surprise and pounced on the unsuspecting Chinese pilots. It became a painful one-sided air duel for the Chinese. The Zeros swarmed over the startled enemy pilots, cutting their aircraft out of the sky with their machine guns and cannon fire. Twenty-seven Russian-made Polikarpov I-15bis biplanes and chunky I-16 monoplane fighters were totally outclassed by the swift and agile Zeros.

In the air battle that lasted a mere 10min, plumes of smoke from fallen Chinese planes filled the sky. When the slaughter ended, the Japanese reported all 27 Chinese fighters destroyed while Chinese records show 16 to 20-plus shot down, crash-landed, or heavily damaged. If there was any disappointment for the Japanese pilots, it was that a few enemy planes were not destroyed until they landed, and one pilot, in his effort to escape, crashed when flying too low to the ground, depriving the Japanese pilots of another aerial target.

Of passing interest, this event on September 13, 1940, happened to be on a Friday as well. According to the Chinese Air Force history, the commander of the Chinese 4th Group that was involved in this encounter was in a hospital that day and expressed foreboding about Friday the Thirteenth. For the Chinese, his premonition came true with disastrous consequences. Not one Zero was lost in this opening air battle, which was the birth of an image of invincibility for the new fighter and for the skill of its pilots. One returning Zero flown by PO 1/C Toraichi Takatsuka had a landing gear malfunction and the aircraft (Tail No. 3-178) was heavily damaged when landing on one wheel. The pilot was not hurt. This malfunction began at takeoff in that the one gear did not fully retract. While hampered in this condition, Takatsuka claimed one I-15 (definite), one I-16, and two I-15 fighters (indefinite).

Japanese bombers could attack at will, with little threat of opposition, because Chinese pilots feared having to engage Zeros. On September 16, a single large Chinese aircraft of an unrecorded type was spotted over the city of Chungking and was immediately shot

down by the six Zeros that were committed to strikes that day. This was the last mission flown in September for these service test aircraft. For the remaining two weeks of that month, mechanics prepared the Zeros for the forthcoming flights that would take them even deeper into enemy territory, where the Chinese Air Force had retreated.

When this small experimental force of Zeros was ready for more combat flying, they were sent on a very long range mission against Chengtu in Szechwan Province on October 4, 1940. Twenty-seven bombers escorted by eight Zeros were to flush out the Chinese at this remote retreat. Again, the attack went unchallenged. As the bombers departed the target area, the formation of Zeros broke off and circled back, undetected, in a wide arc above broken clouds. Bursting in among unsuspecting Chinese pilots flying at Taipingssu airfield, they shot down five Chinese I-16 fighters and one Tupolev medium bomber before strafing the field.

Finding that they were still unopposed, four Zeros led by FWO Higashiyama landed on the airfield. While the remaining pilots in the Zeros overhead provided air cover, the four pilots left their aircraft with engines running, and ran to the Chinese aircraft left undamaged by their strafing attacks. They began setting them on fire until Chinese troops became aware of what was happening. Outnumbered, the Japanese pilots ran for their planes and made a hasty retreat. This legendary, yet foolhardy feat is but one example of the confidence the Zero gave its pilots. Reconnaissance photos later confirmed as

many as 19 aircraft of various types were destroyed on the ground. Only two Zeros received light damage.

The second unit to receive the Zero was the 14th Kokutai in south China. Their A5M4 Claude fighters were supplemented with nine new Zeros on September 1940. With the northern portion of French Indochina (Vietnam) recently occupied by Japanese forces, the 14th Kokutai moved to Gia Lam airfield at Hanoi on October 7, 1940. Their mission was to cut off the supply line to the Chinese forces. On the day of their arrival, seven Zeros under the leadership of Lt. Mitsugu Kofukuda, escorted 27 G3M bombers on strikes against Kunming. In the air engagements that ensued with Chinese I-15bis, I-16s, and Curtiss Hawk fighters, the Japanese claimed 14 victories and four damaged in ground strafing with no losses of their own. (This pre-World War II air combat by Zeros of the 14th Kokutai in south China is generally overshadowed by earlier events of the 12th Kokutai in central China three weeks earlier.)

Because of these deadly encounters, the Chinese considered the Zero to be invincible, and their pilots treated it with such caution that they stopped intercepting . Thus, the Japanese gained air superiority over almost the entire Chinese theater of war. This complete control of the air meant that bombers of all descriptions would be sent on operations deep into Chinese territory at will, protected by the awe-inspiring Zero. During the four months from August 19, 1940, until the end of that year, a total of 153 Zero sorties were flown in 22 missions during which 59 Chinese

Fighter units generally had one chutai *(six to nine aircraft) of Mitsubishi Navy Type 98 Reconnaissance Aircraft (C5M) assigned for target damage assessment, weather and tactical reconnaissance, and pathfinder navigation. Although obsolete in* *appearance with their fixed landing gear, their performance was greater than one would suspect. Allied code name for the aircraft was Babs. (The Army version, Ki-15-II, is shown here.)*

prepare for the Pacific war. Troops were redeployed for this new war. The Zero, at this point, disappeared from the China skies as this responsibility was shifted to the JAAF. Both the 12th and 14th *Kokutais* were disbanded on September 15, 1941, and their aircraft and personnel were reassigned to the two mainland-based fighter units established for the new conflict, the 3rd and the *Tainan Kokutais,* or to carriers and other units.

This removal of Japanese forces in preparation for the Pacific war, together with massive American aid allowed the Chinese to keep going. However, had Japan not expanded the war into Southeast Asia and the Pacific, and thus not drawn America fully into the war, the results could have been different. The Chinese Air Force would have suffered a fate almost as final as that of the Luftwaffe in the closing months of the war in Europe three years later.

For the Zero, this air war over China had been decidedly a one-sided affair. As the

Zero pilots of the 12th Kokutai, *which participated in the Chengtu raid of September 13, 1940, report their success in mastering the skies over China. Vice Adm. Shigetaro Shimada, commander of the China Area Fleet (at left, facing pilots) listens to their accounts during this first combat engagement with enemy fighters.* Shoichi Tanaka

aircraft were shot down and 101 destroyed on the ground without any loss in the Zero force.

The Japanese airmen had their setbacks, however. On February 21, 1941, the JNAF suffered their first loss of a Zero. Pilot CPO Jiro Chono of the 14th *Kokutai* was killed when his Zero was struck by ground fire while attacking Kunming. Chono was an ace, with seven official victories, all of which were achieved while flying A5M Claudes.

From October 1940 to April 1941, the G3M2 Nell bomber squadrons were withdrawn from the mainland for reorganization. During this six-month period, the Zero was the only aircraft that could attack the Chinese on all fronts, since Chinese air units had retreated beyond the effective range of the other Japanese war planes. Meanwhile, the Zero pilots continued to taunt Chinese pilots into combat.

In the early part of 1941, the air war over China followed with consistency the events of 1940. By September of that year, the Zeros had flown 354 sorties and, according to Japanese figures only, had shot down 44 enemy aircraft and damaged 62 more, at the cost of 3 Zeros lost to antiaircraft fire.

By this time in 1941, the Chinese Air Force was rendered totally ineffective. This situation fostered the edict made by Japanese Naval Air Headquarters to withdraw its air units from mainland China in the latter half of 1941 to

感状

進藤海軍大尉指揮セシ
第○○航空隊戦闘機隊

昭和十五年九月十三日長驅四川省
ノ山嶽地帯ヲ突破シテ攻撃機隊ノ
重慶爆撃ヲ掩護シ一時行動ヲ韜晦シ
敵機誘出ニ努メタル後再度重慶上
空ニ進撃シ陸上偵察機ノ協力ニ依
リ敵戦闘機二十七機ヲ發見捕捉シ
勇戦奮闘克ク其ノ全機ヲ確實ニ撃
墜シタルハ武勳顯著ナリ
仍テ茲ニ感状ヲ授與ス
昭和十五年十月三十一日
支那方面艦隊司令長官 嶋田繁太郎 ㊞

The citation presented to those who participated in the Zero's first combat mission reads as follows:
"TO: No. [blank for publication security] Kokutai, Fighter Force Commanded by Navy Lt. Shindo
"On September 13, 1940, this force escorted attack bomber aircraft in the bombing of Chungking, penetrating, at long range, over the mountain ranges of Sczechuan Province, at one time making a seeming maneuver to withdraw in order to draw out enemy aircraft, then penetrating Chungking airspace a second time, and with the cooperation of a land-based reconnaissance aircraft, succeeded in spotting and making contact with 27 enemy fighter aircraft, and through courageous and vigorous combat, definitely shot down all of them, such action being a tremendous feat of arms." In recognition of the foregoing this citation is hereby presented. October 31, 1940 China Area Fleet "Commander in Chief Shigetaro Shimada"

opening of the Pacific war against the United States drew near, Japanese planners had unshaken faith in the Zero's ability against existing American and British aircraft. A few recognized, however, that should such a war be prolonged, the Japanese and their Zero would face an array of weapons whose qualities and quantities could only be surmised. The days of crushing superiority would be short-lived should the ensuing war become a drawn-out affair. Their opening strategy was that of rapid deployment and conquest of preselected territory, sue for peace, and accept territorial compromise, yet achieving greater expansion over that of their current position.

For the war that was about to begin in the Pacific, considerable reorganization took place within the JNAF. Included were two major air units of which Zeros were a part. The First Air Fleet was a seaborne organization, having under its command all of the fleet carriers of the Imperial Navy. It was the First Air Fleet, under the command of Vice

Adm. Chuichi Nagumo, that attacked Pearl Harbor.

The Eleventh Air Fleet was land-based and had under its command practically all the land-based JNAF units that later would operate in the invasion of Southeast Asia. Based in Taiwan, it was this air fleet, commanded by Vice Adm. Nishizo Tsukahara, that conducted the JNAF operations over the Philippines and later the Dutch East Indies. The two main Zero units in these operations were the 3rd and *Tainan Kokutais,* of which combat-seasoned veteran pilots from the former 12th and 14th *Kokutai*s were once assigned.

The Zero pilots aboard the carriers of the First Air Fleet deserve substantial recognition for their flying skill as well. By and large, the carrier pilots were always the best in the JNAF. But after bursting with such dramatic effect on the consciousness of the West at Pearl Harbor, the carrier-based Zeros only met significant air action at certain concentrated, but isolated points in time.

Chinese pilots flying these Polikarpov I-15bis biplane fighters had a chance against Japanese fighters until the advent of the Zero. The 1933 design was one of the best fighters of its day, but it was no match against the advanced technology of the Zero.

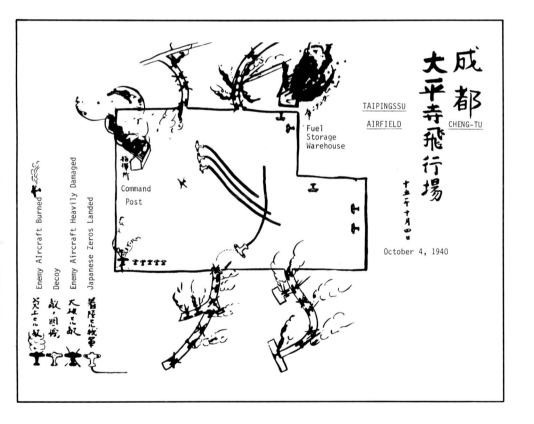

One of the more daring (as well as foolhardy) incidents of the Sino-Japanese war occurred on October 4, 1940. Four frustrated Zero pilots landed their mounts on Taipingssu airfield when no opposition was encountered, and proceeded on foot to destroy Chinese planes on the ground. This post-strike Japanese illustration clearly shows what action took place. Shoichi Tanaka

41

Chapter 7

The War Years

Historians often refer to the predictions made by Japanese planners over their certainty of victory in their initial campaigns of the war. This confidence came because of their unshakable faith that the Zero would control the air over the battle areas. Japanese intelligence and statisticians stated unequivocally that the superiority of the Zero meant that, in battle, one Zero would be the equal of from two to five enemy fighter planes, depending on their type. However, taking into consideration that the potential enemy apparently had unlimited resources, Japanese victories had to be achieved quickly.

For the opening Japanese attack on the US fleet at Pearl Harbor on December 7, 1941, 125 Zeros launched from six Japanese aircraft carriers were involved. The mission of these Zeros, launched in two waves, was not only to provide defensive air cover over the fleet, but 78 were used to escort the bombing aircraft and to strafe American airfields. During the attacks, nine Zeros failed to return to their carriers and were lost, mainly to ground fire.

When the Zeros appeared over Hawaii in the opening phase of the Pacific war, 16 months had passed since their debut in China. The Americans were completely astonished at the sight of the new fighter and were totally unaware of the Zero's performance. Observers in China had submitted reports about the new aircraft, yet they were not heeded.

As recently as the 1987 winter issue of *The Aerospace Historian*, William M. Leary of the University of Georgia tells of the reports made by Gen. Claire Chennault about this startling new Japanese fighter encountered over China. Chennault, a former Army Air Corps officer, was helping to bolster the Chinese Air Force and was organizing the American Volunteer Group (Flying Tigers) when he sent a warning to Washington that few took seriously. This and other reports reached the hands of Army chief of staff Gen. George C. Marshall in late 1940, who in turn made a strong warning to officials at a high-level conference that Japan had a modern fighter aircraft that had literally grounded the Chinese Air Force. Leary points out that Marshall's correspondence of February 1941 to both Lt. Gen. Walter C. Short, commanding general of the Hawaiian defense, and Maj. Gen. George Grunert, commanding general of the Philippines, told very explicitly of the Zero's capability. Eight months before the attack on Pearl Harbor, the *Army Field Manual* on aircraft recognition contained reasonably accurate data on the Zero—but no pictures. One picture of this new fighter may well have made all the difference by visually showing the existence of the fighter being described.

The warning had been made, intelligence services did their part, but it was the *users* of this information that failed to appreciate the significance of the Zero in the event of wartime involvement with the United States.

Fuel tanks are topped off as dawn breaks over Takao Air Base, Taiwan, early December 1941. These Zeros of the 3rd Kokutai are about to depart for their long journey to attack the Philippines. Overnight settling of the fuel tanks allowed space for more fuel by morning. Shoichi Tanaka

The crew of the aircraft carrier Akagi *prepare their ship for the possible counterattack by American aircraft after the Japanese attack on Pearl Harbor, December 7, 1941. The Zero in the foreground has its engine protected from the elements by a snug fitting thermo-covering.* Shoichi Tanaka

The Japanese were equally surprised at Western ignorance after having exposed their Zero for more than a year in air battles over China.

A few hours following the attack upon Hawaii, Clark and Iba air bases in the Philippines (December 8 local time) were left in burning rubble by Japanese bombers escorted by Zeros of the 3rd and *Tainan Kokutais.* The Americans were convinced that the fighters had been launched from nearby aircraft carriers, which was originally the way the Japanese plan intended. Instead, after confirming the long range of the Zero, 89 of these fighters struck targets in the Philippines, all of which flew the round-trip mission from bases on Tai-

wan. This was a distance of 934nm, round-trip, and also allowed fuel for combat engagements over the target area. The Zero's range was put to the ultimate test and in turn freed the aircraft carriers for other strikes.

It should be mentioned here that this plan for striking from distant land bases rather than using aircraft carriers was not just happenstance. The Japanese Navy had learned well from the British training of the early 1920s that an effective naval air arm must not be totally dependent upon aircraft carriers in fulfilling its mission. Therefore, land-based aircraft with longer range must be a major design consideration. In support of this concept, extensive functional flights were made by pilots of the 3rd and *Tainan Kokutais* in October and November 1941 in preparation for the attack on the Philippines. This point, made famous by Saburo Sakai's books about the Zero, told how pilots learned techniques that would extend the officially recognized range of the Zero. This exceptional range became a key factor in

the success that the Zero enjoyed throughout the war.

Of the few aircraft that rose to defend the Philippine bases on this first of many attacks, none was a match for the Zero. The only US fighter force on the Philippines at that time was the 24th Pursuit Group with Curtiss P-40Bs and Es and Seversky P-35As. Strafing and bombing attacks destroyed many American aircraft, including half the B-17 Flying Fortresses (12 destroyed) and a quarter of their fighters (35 destroyed) based in the Philippines. Zero losses came to seven aircraft.

Frequent Japanese raids on the Philippines followed, and by December 13, after five days of attack, the US air forces had been virtually annihilated in that area. This was due in large measure to the Zeros of the 3rd and *Tainan Kokutais.* This aerial blitz on the Philippines firmly established the Zero's reputation among its enemies.

After some preliminary landings on the northern and southern coastlines of the Philip-

This is the sprawling base at Takao, Taiwan, at which the 3rd Kokutai was based at the beginning of the Pacific War. It was from here that Zeros from this unit attacked the Philippines on their non-stop extended-range mission. Most of these Zeros have their engines running in preparation for their take-off on December 8, 1941. Their mission was to attack Iba and Clark airfields after escorting land-based bombers to their targets. Shoichi Tanaka

Intent on the early morning takeoff from the carrier Akagi, this pilot guides his A6M2 down the wooden deck for the attack on Pearl Harbor. Of the 125 Zeros that took part in this attack, only nine failed to return. Shoichi Tanaka

pines, Zeros of one *chutai* of the *Tainan Kokutai* moved from Taiwan on December 14, to the newly captured Legaspi airfield. From there they shared the air battle with JAAF units already operating from Vigan and Aparri airfields. The main Japanese assault force went ashore at Lingayen Gulf on December 22. On the southernmost island of the Philippines, the 3rd *Kokutai* began its move from Takao, Taiwan, to Davao air base on Mindanao. By December 29 the Japanese had total air superiority over all of the Philippines, although limited American air operations continued out of Del Monte until mid-April 1942.

From their new base at Davao, on December 28, the 3rd *Kokutai* launched its first air missions to the south in further conquests. Seven Zeros in company with a land-based reconnaissance aircraft attacked the distant island of Tarakan (520nm) on the northeast

Right

At the beginning of the Pacific War and before, JNAF pilots were among the best trained in the world. An accelerated training program was never thought necessary for meeting the combat losses that ensued. As a result, the wartime pilot training program was forced to send under-trained Japanese pilots to face well-trained American pilots in the latter stages of the war. Shown here is a formation training flight over Ohita Air Base, Kyushu, early in the war. Shoichi Tanaka

At Takao Air Base, Taiwan, ground crewmen of the 3rd Kokutai *wave to their Zero fighters departing for their attack on the Philippines on December* 8, 1941. Other Zeros of the 3rd stand on the flight line. Shoichi Tanaka

US Marine pilots of VMF-211. This engagement was the first of many between the Zero and the F4F Wildcat.

To deny the use of these eastern islands to their enemy was a matter of territorial perimeter protection, but Japan's real objectives were the mineral-rich Netherlands East Indies to the south. With the support of the JNAF through January and February 1942, strong amphibious forces leapfrogged southward through the islands toward the heart of the Dutch colonial empire on Java. This consisted of two main lines of advancement, one to the east down the string of islands, and one to the west, primarily along the Malayan peninsula.

Air cover for the eastern arm of the advance was the responsibility of the JNAF, and it was along this route that both the 3rd and the *Tainan Kokutais* participated. Within this eastern corridor of the Japanese advance, the line of movement was also split, having the *Tainan Kokutai* on the western side of the islands while the 3rd went down the eastern side. Thus the *Tainan Kokutai* went from Taiwan to Jolo Island (a detachment having operated earlier at Legaspi in the central Philip-

The early morning hours of December 7, 1941, found these Zero Fighters aboard the flag ship Akagi, *warming-up their engines in preparation for their attack on Hawaii. In this opening attack force on the US fleet at Pearl Harbor, 78 of the 125 Zeros aboard six aircraft carriers were involved.* Shoichi Tanaka

coast of Borneo. During this mission, Dutch fighters were encountered for the first time. They had little chance of even engaging the Zeros because the Japanese pilots took the initiative and jumped nine Dutch Brewster Buffaloes while in the process of taking off. The Zeros shot down three without a loss to themselves.

While the action was going well for the Japanese in this part of the Pacific, operations did not go as planned elsewhere. In the opening phase of the war, a fleet landing assault on Wake Island had air support only by unescorted G3M Nell bombers flying out of Kwajalein in the Marshall Islands. This operation was vigorously repulsed by the US Marine defenders of Wake, to the great embarrassment of the Japanese. From the returning carrier force used for the attack on Pearl Harbor, the carriers *Soryu* and *Hiryu* were diverted and placed in support of this operation. With this help from the carrier aircraft, including Zeros, the second assault brought about the surrender of Wake Island to the Japanese. In this struggle by the few surviving defenders, Zero pilot FPO 3/C Isao Tahara from the carrier *Hiryu* quickly shot down the remaining two American fighters in the often told heroic action by

This Zero did not get away. Nine Zeros failed to return to their carriers after the crushing attacks on Pearl Harbor on December 7. These losses were mainly attributed to antiaircraft fire. National Archives

One of the Japanese losses during the attacks on Hawaii was this A6M2, s/n 5289, from the aircraft carrier Akagi. *The aircraft's crashed remains found at Fort Kamehameha were moved to this hangar for a closer look at Japanese aircraft technology.*

pines), then to Tarakan Island off Borneo's east coast, to Balikpapan on Borneo, and finally to Bali.

The 3rd *Kokutai* went from Taiwan to Davao on the southern Philippine island of Mindanao, then to Menado on the northeastern tip of Celebes. After that, it sent detachments to Kendari in southeastern Celebes, Balikpapan, Makassar, and Ambon, ultimately concentrating at Koepang on Timor.

The western portion of the assault toward Java was primarily an Imperial Japanese Army operation. The advancing JNAF unit that joined in this assault—drawn from personnel of both the 3rd and *Tainan Kokutais* just prior to the start of the war—never had a proper independent designation and was known simply as "Fighter Group attached to 22nd Air Flotilla Headquarters." They proceeded down the Malayan Peninsula for the capture of Singapore, together with supporting landings on Borneo's western coast, then on to Sumatra and ultimately the invasion of western Java. Air cover for this western advance was predominantly the responsibility of the JAAF, although one Zero formation did take part in that campaign, along with the Army's Oscars and Nates.

There were many noteworthy air engagements over Singapore, which included this group of Zeros, when Japanese pilots engaged British defenders. One occurred on January 22, 1942, when nine Zeros were escorting G3M Nells and G4M Bettys on a bombing raid. The bomber formations were attacked by 12 RAF Hawker Hurricanes, to which the nine Zeros gave chase. When the brief air battle ended, the Zeros had bagged five Hurricanes. Conflicting information on Japanese losses indicates two Zeros lost but with pilots recovered, while other sources indicate no Japanese losses.

Over Surabaya, Java, on February 3, 1942, 27 Zeros led by Lt. Tamotsu Yokoyama of the 3rd *Kokutai*, with another 27 Zeros from the *Tainan Kokutai*, engaged Dutch and American

Ground crews cheer their pilots of the 3rd Kokutai as they taxi out for takeoff from Takao airfield, Taiwan. This is the start of an early raid on the Philippines at the beginning of the Pacific war. Shoichi Tanaka

pilots in a major air battle. Contrary to previous engagements, the Allied pilots were already airborne and waiting over the city for the arrival of the Japanese attackers. The battle that followed was vicious and costly. The Japanese claimed 39 enemy aircraft shot down and 21 severely damaged on the ground or set on fire. Allied claims, on the other hand, reported eight Curtiss-Wright CW-21B Interceptors, and three Curtiss Hawk 75s (similar to P-36s) downed with a loss of three Zeros and one C5M Babs reconnaissance aircraft. Regardless of the true count, both sides recognized this air battle as one of the largest and most significant of the Java campaign. It ended with a clear victory for the Zero.

Later, on March 1, 1942, the 3rd *Kokutai* with six Zeros was back over Blimbing, Java. This time, the US 17th Pursuit Squadron (Provisional) was caught off guard at their base on eastern Java. The Zeros strafed the American P-40Es and destroyed 14 of the Kittyhawks. This marked the end of US fighter and heavy bomber operations in Java. The Dutch surrendered on March 9.

Japanese probes were made even farther south to Port Darwin, Australia, the first of which came from four of Admiral Nagumo's aircraft carriers on February 19, 1942. This was a devastating raid brought about by 188 attacking aircraft. The docks and shipyards, loaded with supplies for Allied forces, suffered heavy losses. Defending pilots in Curtiss P-40Es did everything they could with their limited combat experience, but the raiding aircraft that included 36 Zeros was too much for them. In the battle, the 33rd Pursuit Squadron (Provisional), lost ten P-40s to the Japanese. Before departing, the Zeros caused further damage by strafing the build-up of combat materials at the port. One Zero was lost due to ground fire.

Attacks that followed against Australia were flown from land bases. Zeros provided air cover for each of these operations during which they maintained air superiority, but American resistance was becoming more tenacious and skilled. For this Australian campaign, Zeros and other Japanese aircraft flew from bases on Timor Island, 400nm to the northwest. The Allies still failed to grasp the true capabilities of the Zero, to cover such dis-

By the end of December 1941, the 3rd Kokutai moved to their new base at Davao in the southern Philippines, where they were within striking distance of the Celebes Islands. This formation of Zeros over the Celebes in early 1942 may well have been against Kendari, their next base of operations. Shoichi Tanaka

When the Japanese occupied the airstrip at Del Monte, in the Philippines, they discovered the remains of damaged B-17s of the 19th Bomb Group. They repaired one B-17D and two B-17Es for flight to Japan where they were evaluated. H. Nagakubo

Early morning work for these mechanics: a hurried spark plug change for this A6M2 of the 3rd Kokutai in time for its next scheduled sortie. Forces of the 3rd were dispersed for making widespread attacks from bases like this on Bali Island, Dutch East Indies, in early March 1941. Shoichi Tanaka

tances and then function so well as a fighter in the air duels that followed.

These land-based Zero units racked up an astounding record during the opening months of fighting. For instance, the Eleventh Air Fleet, under the direction of Admiral Tsukahara, made claim of shooting down 565 enemy aircraft from the opening day of the Pacific war to the close of the Java operation in early March 1942. Of this number, Zeros were credited for 471 victories, or 83 percent of the total. As history so often reveals when comparing the accounts of both sides, Allied victories and losses would logically vary widely from these figures, mainly based on double claims made in the heat of battle. But it is evident, regardless of the exact totals, that the Zero reigned supreme. The Zero's range allowed the Japanese to set the time and place for engaging their enemy, often catching the meager Allied forces off guard. The unexpected appearance of the Zero in forceful numbers gave the Zero its reputation of being every-

Eleven victory markings on the tail of a Zero. This A6M2 belonged to the 3rd Kokutai when operating out of Bali, and by this time was assigned to Naval Air Pilot 2/C Yoshiro Hashiguchi. The turned rudder is darkened by its own shadow. Shoichi Tanaka

Island conquest by the advancing Japanese was rapid in the early months of the war. This view shows a Zero of the 3rd Kokutai being refueled at the newly captured base at Kendari, on Celebes Is- *land, east of Borneo. From here, the main force continued its move to Balikpapan, Borneo. Shoichi Tanaka*

where through the war zone, and a force to be reckoned with.

Japanese advances had been so successful, far beyond the wildest imaginations of Japan's

With the capture of Kupang on Timor Island, elements of the 3rd Kokutai began operating from nearby Burton airfield starting on February 23, 1942, where this picture was taken. Parked in protective revetments, the open canopies on these Zeros are shielded by canvas coverings to protect them from the tropical heat. Shoichi Tanaka

military strategists, that by January 1942, plans were expanded to include taking all of Burma. For implementing the operation that began in late March, five of Admiral Nagumo's carriers swept far into the Indian Ocean, escorted by fast, modern battleships and numerous other warships. Their mission was to strike British naval bases on the island of Ceylon (Sri Lanka) and to destroy any British warships and merchant vessels they could find in the Indian Ocean and Bay of Bengal. This was to ease the Japanese Army's invasion of Burma with landings from the sea.

When the operation began on April 5, 1942, more than 200 Japanese carrier planes, including 36 Zeros, hit the British naval base at Colombo on Ceylon. They were met by about 60 RAF aircraft of assorted types, many of which were obsolete. A violent air battle took place over the southwestern part of the island, with the RAF being the heavier loser of 27 aircraft. Shot down were 15 Hawker Hurricanes, eight Fairey Swordfish and four Fairey Fulmars, to that of a single Zero.

Typical forward-base flight-line view of Zero strength with their Babs photo reconnaissance aircraft in the foreground. This was Kendari, one of the forward bases for the 3rd Kokutai, on southern Celebes Island. It was not unusual for fighter units to have their own pre- and post-strike reconnaissance element within their unit. Shoichi Tanaka

Zeros from the carrier Soryu take a brief rest at Kendari Air Base in the Celebes Islands, Indonesia, in March 1942. They had participated in the attack on Darwin, Australia, the previous month. From Kendari, this force of Zeros went aboard the Soryu once again, this time headed for Indian Ocean operations. Shoichi Tanaka

On April 9, the Japanese carrier force returned to Ceylon, this time to strike the naval base at Trincomalee on the northern tip. Once again, the RAF was waiting. While this air battle was taking place over the target area, a few British light bombers attacked the Japanese carriers, but most were repelled by Zeros. One Kate and three Zeros were lost in exchange for eight Hawker Hurricanes and three Fairey Fulmars.

Even during this period of unquestionable Japanese superiority (December 1941 to March 1942), however, the Zero quickly revealed its vulnerability to gunfire. Even in the first day of the Pacific war, some Zeros were shot down by obsolete Curtiss P-36s over Pearl Harbor and by P-40s over the Philippines. So long as the quality of Japanese naval fighter pilots remained high, however, such instances remained rare. These skilled pilots were able to capitalize on the Zero's design philosophy—one of foregoing aircraft protective features in order to enhance performance so that the aircraft could fly its way out of trouble. The Zero pilots of the early war period seldom gave their opponents the chance to get a good shot at them. But even the best of pilots can have an inattentive moment or a split second of indecision. If he is unlucky and becomes the target of a stream of .50cal fire, all the skill and experience will not stop the bullets from piercing the cockpit or unprotected fuel tanks.

As Japan's conquests led to further expansion of its area of control, Allied fighter pilots

Typical of any air force, this flight of three Zeros of the 3rd Kokutai buzz Burton airfield at Kupang on Timor Island following a successful air strike. This Kokutai was one of the participating air units responsible for the sinking of the American seaplane tender USS Langley. Shoichi Tanaka

began to take the Zero's measure. They found that although they could not turn with the Zero, they could out-dive it. What American fighters lacked in performance versus the Zero, they made up for in ruggedness of construction. Mutually protective tactical formations and hit-and-run attacks became the order of the day. The occasions on which relatively inexperienced American pilots scored against the Zero began to increase.

It can be argued that Japan had won the war it set out to fight once Java was occupied, but it had not considered how to maintain the victory. Japanese tacticians had a vague notion that once their objective of capturing the vast oil and mineral resources of Southeast Asia had been attained, they could consolidate their gains, fight America and its Allies to a stalemate, and then negotiate an end to the war.

Instead, the anger of the Americans over the Pearl Harbor attack and the Japanese conquest of the Philippines made an Allied counterattack a certainty. Recognizing these possibilities in January and February 1942, before the completion of the Java invasion, Japanese planners saw the necessity for a buffer zone around their vital interests. To provide this security, they considered the capture of such places as Port Moresby in Papua New Guinea, Midway Island, the Aleutians, and others imperative. This would increase Allied supply lines to an almost unthinkable distance. In pursuit of these objectives, each battle had a unique set of combat circumstances in which the Zero was involved, some battles quite decisive, others a narrow victory or defeat.

After the fall of the Netherlands East Indies, the 3rd *Kokutai* remained in the area. Up to this time, March 1942, it was the 3rd that had seen the greatest share of air-to-air combat, putting to great advantage their seasoned veterans from the China conflict. Their sister unit, the *Tainan Kokutai*, was transferred to Rabaul on New Britain, and to the forward base at Lae, New Guinea, arriving in mid-

April 1942. It was this group that was about to become the dominant Zero unit in the Pacific theater. Throughout the vast new Japanese empire, action became intensive only in this area, which the Allies referred to as the Southwest Pacific. Burma and China, a Japanese Army responsibility, remained quiet, relatively speaking, as were the northern and central Pacific.

From April to August 1942, Zeros of the *Tainan Kokutai* were at the peak of their power. In rapid succession they fought and prevailed over the Curtiss Kittyhawks of No. 75 Squadron, RAAF, and the P-39 and P-400 Airacobras of the US 8th and 35th Fighter Groups. They also fought B-17s of the 19th Bomb Group, the B-26 Marauders of the 22nd Bomb Group, the B-25s and A-24s of the 3rd Bomb Group, as well as other units. Zeros maintained a solid air superiority over Eastern New Guinea and the Bismarck Archipelago throughout this period, although Allied pressure was building. This was the Zero at its best.

The Japanese military conquest went unchecked over the vast area of the Pacific and its many islands until the concentrated naval engagement in the Coral Sea on May 7–8, 1942. A Japanese task force was on its way toward New Guinea with the intent of an

This rare photograph from the carrier deck shows a Zero Model 32 taking off, possibly on a strike mission in the Southwest Pacific. Air engagements with carrier-based Zeros were far less frequent than with those based on land, which saw action almost daily. Shoichi Tanaka

A squadron strength of Zeros belonging to the Tainan Kokutai taxi for takeoff from this airfield at Lae, New Guinea. This was a forward base from their main airfield on Rabaul. Attacks originating from here were primarily against Port Moresby. Shoichi Tanaka

invasion at Port Moresby. Elsewhere, Adm. Frank Fletcher's US Navy task force was reforming at sea, intent on intercepting the Japanese. Erroneous ship spotting on both sides sent opposing formations of attacking aircraft after scattered ships of the two fleets. Not one enemy surface craft engaged another, but what ensued was the first carrier-vs.-carrier battle in history. Wave after wave of aircraft fought bitterly against their enemy. When the encounter ended, the Japanese had lost their light carrier *Shoho* and suffered damage to their fleet carrier *Shokaku*, while the US fleet carrier *Lexington* had sunk. The Japanese claimed victory over this engagement, however, the Americans won the strategic victory: The US Navy had stopped the seaborne invasion of Port Moresby on the southern coast of Papua New Guinea.

Using the Zero for night air defense against attacking enemy bombers was not uncommon, but was not overly productive either. They did have their effect upon the attacking bomber crews and did score a number of victories. This Model 32 begins taxiing from the flight line for what may be an early morning takeoff in readiness for daylight air operations.

Adm. Isoroku Yamamoto was a strong supporter of the air arm of the Imperial Japanese Navy. This photo, taken at Lakunai airfield, Rabaul, on New Britain Island, shows the admiral watching flight operations a mere four days before his fateful demise on April 18, 1943. Shoichi Tanaka

During the two-day battle, the Zeros fought ruthlessly. The situation was not a matter of supremacy of one fighter over another, but of one aerial force over another. This opening engagement of carrier-based Zeros opposing carrier-based Wildcats emphasized the strong need for tactics to counter the Zero's superior maneuverability.

By June 1942, the Japanese fleet, supported by its contingent of Zeros, attempted to invade Midway Island. This was Japan's planned second stage of expansion; it hoped to use the invasion of Midway to lure the US Pacific Fleet into a decisive battle and later, after the island's capture, use it as a base for raids on Hawaii.

The Japanese thought they had the element of surprise on their side, but the Americans were prepared for the attack. The battle started favorably for the Japanese when they successfully defended their carriers against attack and the American forces took heavy aerial losses at the hands of the Zero pilots and heavy shelling from the ships. But, as the battle progressed and the Japanese turned their attention to the low-flying US torpedo bombers attacking their ships, US dive-bombers came in steeply overhead and unloaded their 1,000 pound bombs, many of them squarely on the Japanese carriers. Three were sunk and a fourth was set on fire and was scuttled. With them went 234 Japanese aircraft, most of the Zeros being lost when they made crash-landings in the sea for lack of mother ships.

When considering the results of the air battle that took place, a fairly clear pattern

Land-based fighter units often operated from dirt strips. Seldom were hard surfaces available. Typical was this setting at Kupang on the southwest end of Timor Island in the spring of 1942. This A6M2 belongs to the 3rd Kokutai. Shoichi Tanaka

began to emerge in Allied tactics. Those who chose to dogfight the Zero would be soundly defeated. Those who chose to use what superior qualities they had in their aircraft with better protective features would at least hold their own against the A6M Zero. To heed the sound lesson of "Do not dogfight with the Zero" was often the deciding factor between victory or defeat for Allied pilots. Instead, hitting hard and fast, followed by breaking the engagement, was often the key to success.

Carrier-based fighter pilots were among the best in the JNAF. Their involvement in combat was limited to infrequent sea engagements, while those from the land-based fighter units were in combat on nearly a daily basis.

Two versions of the A6M3 Zero taxi out for takeoff at an airfield near Rabaul. In the lead is the clipped-wing Model 32, followed by the longer-wing Model 22. It was not unusual for the various Kokutais to fly a mission with a mixed bag of Zero models. Shoichi Tanaka

In this raid on Midway Island, the Zeros downed 13 land-based F2A Buffalos and two F4F-3 Wildcats of VMF-221 for the loss of no more than one or two Zeros. By contrast, the Navy F4F-4s of the carrier units did very well. Lt. Comdr. Jimmy Thach and his division of four Wildcats fought upwards of 20 Zeros, and for the loss of one plane and pilot, claimed upwards of five Zeros in an epic battle. This was the first test in combat of his famous "Thach Weave," whereby one fighter protects the blind-spot of the other.

While some historians look upon this battle as the turning point of the war in disfavor of Japan, it was clearly the end of Japan's central Pacific offensive. The loss of Japanese carriers made future large-scale air-sea operations difficult. The aircrews, however, were by no means annihilated. They took heavy losses,

to be sure, but many survived the battle to be reassigned to other units. To the south, in New Guinea, the Japanese remained on the offensive.

The only Japanese accomplishment during the Battle of Midway was the seizing of the tiny, uninhabited islands of Attu and Kiska in the far-off Aleutians, and this was partially a diversionary effort. The apparent gain produced a greater loss to the Japanese, for it was from this northern operation zone that the Americans acquired a downed Zero and discovered, for the first time, its innermost secrets.

Turned back in their seaward invasion of Port Moresby by the Battle of the Coral Sea, the Japanese landed at Buna in mid-July 1942, on the northeastern coast of New Guinea. They refurbished and expanded the pre-existing airstrip there to support the invasion. This intrusion by the Japanese led to some of the fiercest fighting in air combat up to that time. As the Allies tried to repel the Japanese with P-39 Airacobras and P-40 Warhawks, they were confronted by some of the greatest Zero pilot aces of the JNAF. Despite these Allied efforts, the Japanese were able to mount a drive

southward over the Owen Stanley Mountains toward Port Moresby. Their efforts ended in retreat, however, due to a necessary diversion of resources needed to counter the US invasion of Guadalcanal.

To the east on Guadalcanal in the southern Solomon Islands, the Japanese had begun construction of an airfield the previous June. The purpose was to consolidate their hold on the Solomons and the Coral Sea. While intent on their own land offensive against Port Moresby, the Japanese were taken completely by surprise when US Marines landed on Guadalcanal on August 7, 1942, and captured their nearly completed airfield. This was the first major attempt by the Americans to strike back at the Japanese. The combined air, land, and sea assault by the Allies started the long road to recovering lost ground.

To counter this invasion, the 25th Air Flotilla headquartered at Rabaul sent 17 A6M2 Zeros of the *Tainan Kokutai* based there, as escort for 27 G4M Betty bombers to attack the American beachhead. The unheard of distance of 560nm—each way—was flown by these fighters, a greater distance than the Taiwan-to-Philippines raids. The Japanese were to dis-

This early-model Zero, A6M2, kicks up dust as it lands at its home base near Rabaul in early 1943. It may have just returned from a mission over distant Guadalcanal. Heat, insects, fatigue, poor food, and unshakable illnesses plagued Japanese pilots throughout the South Pacific.

rupt, if not avert, the US landing forces in their landing operations. In their opening attempt, they were met by opposing US Navy F4F Wildcats from the carriers USS *Enterprise* and USS *Saratoga*. The inevitable air battle that developed accounted for eight Wildcats being shot down (some sources indicate 11) and one

SBD Dauntless. The Japanese lost two Zeros and five Bettys. This was the air engagement in which fighter ace FPO 1/C Saburo Sakai was seriously wounded. His flight back to Rabaul was one of the epic flights of the Pacific war, made famous by his book *Samurai* (with Martin Caidin and Fred Saito, New York: E. P. Dutton and Company, Inc., 1957).

The six-month land, sea, and air campaign for Guadalcanal was attrition warfare on a huge scale, the kind that Japan could ill afford. Many *Tainan Kokutai* aces and veteran pilots fell in battle. From August to the end of October 1942, the *Kokutai* lost 32 pilots. Caught by the American landings with no interim airfield between Rabaul and Guadalcanal, the Zeros

were forced to operate at the extreme limit of their range. (Interim airstrips at Buin on Bougainville and Munda on New Georgia did not become ready until October and December 1942, respectively.)

For Japanese pilots, there was always the hope that their more advanced fighter once again would give them an edge over Allied aviators. Instead, as if Zero pilots did not already have enough to contend with for the long-distance and tiring flight from Rabaul to Guadalcanal and the combat engaged there, they were now faced with a new enemy aircraft, the Lockheed P-38 Lightning . Beginning on November 18, 1942, the 339th Fighter Squadron, 347 Fighter Group, based at Hen-

derson Field on Guadalcanal, became the first Lightning squadron to fire its guns in anger at the Zeros. The P-38 combined long range with heavy firepower. Against the nimble Zero, however, the P-38 could only succeed with hit-and-run tactics. Faced with these new fighters and fresh, yet well-trained pilots, the myth about the Zero's invincibility was fading rapidly.

Having been in continuous action from April 1942 onward in the Pacific theater, the pilots of the *Tainan Kokutai* were now victims of battle fatigue. Their unit was finally pulled out of the conflict and transferred to Japan for rest and re-forming in mid-November 1942. By this time, the unit had less than 20 surviving pilots. The unit as a whole for this campaign claimed 201 enemy aircraft shot down, of which 37 were probables. The cost of these victories was 32 highly skilled Zero pilots.

Meanwhile, Japanese reinforcements were rushed to the theater. Besides the 2nd *Kokutai* (582nd *Daitai*), with their newly assigned A6M3s which arrived August 6, 1942 (the day before the US landing on Guadalcanal), the 6th *Kokutai* sent an advanced contingent of Zeros in late August. The remainder of the unit arrived in early October. The 3rd *Kokutai* sent a detachment to operate temporarily under the *Tainan Kokutai* command from September to early November.

Mid-September saw the arrival of the *Kanoya Kokutai,* primarily a bomber unit equipped with Bettys, but with an attached squadron of Zeros. (Later, this Zero squadron was expanded and became an independent, all-fighter unit, the 253rd *Kokutai*.) In addition,

A Zero Model 22 is just breaking ground as it departs Lakunai airfield at Rabaul, referred to as East Field by the Japanese. These new and improved versions of the shorter-wing Model 32 engaged in fierce battle over Guadalcanal as the Americans began their counteroffensive to regain the island. Shoichi Tanaka

Elements of the Zuikaku Sentoki-Tai *operated from Bougainville Island during January and February 1943. The unit claimed about 40 victories while assisting in aerial cover operations for Japanese evacuating units from Guadalcanal.* Juzo Nakamura via James F. Lansdale

Although the markings of these A6M2s have been retouched for censorship, these Zeros are known to belong to the 3rd Kokutai. These aircraft operated north of Australia—possibly from Timor—in the opening months of 1942. Overhead is a Betty bomber seemingly cut out of the pattern by landing Zeros.

This mix of A6M2s (foreground) and A6M3 Model 22s are preparing for takeoff from Kahili airstrip near Buin, on Bougainville. Their mission is in support of the Solomon Islands Campaign.

the 252nd *Kokutai* arrived in early November. Air components from some carriers operated temporarily for short periods from land bases around Rabaul while the carriers returned to Japan for refitting and repairs. Included were Zeros from *Shokaku* and *Zuikaku* that arrived from late August to early September at Buka, north of Bougainville, and from the carrier *Hiyo* in late October to mid-December at Rabaul and Buin, Bougainville.

Many Zero units converged on this theater of operations during late 1942 and in 1943, but

none served as long and as continuously as the 204th *Kokutai*. Initially known as the 6th *Kokutai* until renumbered in November 1942, it was active in the Southwest Pacific from August 1942 until withdrawn to Truk in the central Pacific in late January 1944. This period from April 1942 until mid-February 1944, when most aircraft were finally withdrawn from Rabaul, constitutes the longest continuous air campaign of the Pacific war, and the 204th fought continuously. Their unit claim was about 1,000 enemy aircraft shot down.

The fight above Guadalcanal introduced another new fighter into the arena, this being the US Navy's Vought F4U-1 Corsair. Their baptism to combat came on February 14, 1943, when VMF-124 launched its Corsairs in conjunction with an assortment of American P-

40s and P-38s escorting PB4Y-1 Liberators as these bombers attacked Kahili aerodrome in central Solomons. An estimated 50 Zeros attacked the bombers and the melee began. The score ended with four P-38s down, as well as two each of the P-40s, Corsairs, and Liberators. Only three or four Zeros were bagged in the fight, one being involved in a mid-air collision with a disabled Corsair.

Another Allied fighter came into the Pacific action, the Republic P-47 Thunderbolt. P-47s first engaged JAAF Ki-43 Oscars over New Guinea on August 16, 1943, but it was not until the following September that the Zero met Thunderbolts in combat for the first time. The P-47 was no match to the Zero in maneuverability, but the Zero's advantages ended there. The P-47 was more than twice

A flight of Marine F4U-1 Corsairs taxis out on the fighter strip on Bougainville in February 1944. They will join with a formation of bombers to be escorted to Rabaul, where the certainty is high that they will engage protective Zeros. USMC 77839

as heavy as the Zero and thus more durable, had twice the horsepower, and twice the firepower.

Some relief came to the JNAF pilots when the more advanced A6M5 Zero Model 52 arrived in the Pacific in October 1943. Its increased engine power gave it some improvement in performance, but at the penalty of reduced range. Its survivability had been improved with thicker skin in critical areas, which in turn allowed for an increase in diving speed. This was a critical factor when pitted against the heavier and faster diving American fighters.

No sooner had this advanced version been placed into combat in the Pacific, than it encountered the US Navy's new Grumman F6F Hellcat. The first engagement occurred on Oc-

Years following the war, this relic of an A6M2 was found and photographed on Bougainville, possibly near Buin. The ravages of time and salt air have all but destroyed the airplane. The islands have many such remembrances of the past. M. Clayton

tober 5, 1943 (October 6 in Japan), when US carriers launched a raid on Japanese-occupied Wake Island. In the ensuing battle, 47 Hellcats from the carriers USS *Essex, Yorktown*, the new *Lexington* and *Cowpens* tangled with a total of 26 Zeros of a mixed variety from the 252nd *Kokutai*. The Japanese claimed ten American planes shot down and lost 16 aircraft (actual) of their own. Americans claimed 22 Japanese planes destroyed, with six US losses (actual). The Hellcat was the victor by count, yet each side had hoped to gain greater superiority with their improved fighters.

There were many air battles during the months that followed, in which the Zero was often present. Other *Kokutais* sending their Zeros into battle included the 201st, 251st, and 253rd, to name a few.

One of the most discussed conflicts is the Battle of the Philippine Sea. Combat erupted on June 19, 1944, when the Japanese fleet attempted to counter the Allied invasion of the Mariana Islands. The Japanese task force west of the islands, consisting of nine aircraft carriers and other major ships, had prepared for shuttle attacks against the invading American task force that was positioned between the Japanese fleet and the Japanese-held islands. Shortly after dawn on June 19, the Japanese carriers began sending their Zeros on a strike mission against the American ships and landing assault forces. Foreseeing the Japanese

The A6M5, an improved model and generally the last development of the Zero. It arrived in the combat zone about October 1943, just as the new American heavy fighters joined the fight. Refinements to this model included short exhaust stacks for added thrust effect. USAF 28886 AC

This airstrip on Tarawa in the Gilberts reveals the heavy fighting that took place there in November 1943. The defeated and the victors are evident in this picture, with an A6M2 Zero in the foreground and a Marine F6F Hellcat landing after a mission. USMC 65611

plan, the F6F Hellcats were already waiting high above the fleet. As the Japanese planes appeared, the American fighters dove down upon them in a devastating, coordinated attack.

Over a period of 8hr, four successive waves of Japanese planes flew in from the southwest, one group numbering about one hundred aircraft. The same fate was experienced by each wave. Only about 40 of the Japanese aircraft got through the defending fighters, and half of these were shot down by the ships' curtain of intense antiaircraft fire.

About 370 Japanese planes were shot down during this spectacular aerial battle which history refers to as the Marianas Turkey Shoot. Counting the land-based Japanese planes that took off for the islands earlier that morning and were shot down, total Japanese losses for the day were more than 400 aircraft. Of the original 450 Japanese planes used during the battle, only 1 in 10 had survived. On the remaining carriers, only six torpedo-bombers, two dive-bombers, 12 attack-bombers, and a mere 25 of the original complement of 225 Zeros remained. Twenty-six American planes were lost.

These results, of course, were very one-sided because the increased performance of the upgraded zeros was gravely offset by new Allied fighters piloted by fresh, well-trained aviators versus the deteriorating skill of Japanese pilots. Whether it was due to Japanese tactical error, or because of the poor state of training of the Japanese pilots for an operation of this size, the attack came in widely separated and ill-coordinated waves. This allowed the American aircraft time to reservice and rearm. The Japanese pilots were also in a semi-exhausted state after flying nearly 350nm from their carriers, supposedly out of reach of US planes, and were therefore at a disadvantage in evading the fierce and overwhelming attacks.

The eventual capture of Saipan by the Allied invasion force placed in American hands 21 Zeros in fair condition and seven spare engines. About 12 of the latest Zero models were sent to the United States for flight evaluation.

Once the Allied forces broke through the Japanese strongholds of the Bismarck Archipelago with the capture of the Admiralty Islands in February 1944, they advanced rapidly in a series of bold, leap-frogging operations. Hollandia, New Guinea, fell in April 1944, followed by Biak Island in May, and Sansapor, West New Guinea by the end of July. Morotai Island, farther north, was invaded by the Allies in September, the last step before MacArthur's return to the Philippines.

It took only seven months to cover this vast distance. The Philippine campaign of 1944–1945, which began with landings in October, was concluded by January 1945. In contrast to all these phases of the Pacific war, the air campaign over eastern New Guinea, the

Bismarck Archipelago, and the Solomon Islands lasted almost a full two years and consisted of nearly constant combat.

It is the two-year period from April 1942 to April 1944 that proves to be of most historical interest. The two opposing forces were closely matched in many aspects: in the numbers of aircraft available and their relative performance, and the relative skill of the pilots. One must reserve the highest respect for the Allied pilots who stopped the Japanese advance during this period. They did so in aircraft whose performance was not greatly superior to that of the Zero, flying against highly skilled opponents, and at a time when Allied numerical superiority had not yet become overwhelming. In contrast, the Allied pilots of 1944–1945 simply did not often encounter superior, well-trained fighter pilots. They flew

aircraft in greater numbers with a clear performance edge over the Japanese Zero. In addition, the Allies had a working resupply system, something nearly impossible to achieve for the Japanese.

Similarly, the Zero's early victories were usually against aircraft of inferior performance, flown by inexperienced Allied crews, and few in number. Increasingly during the latter half of 1942 and throughout 1943, however, Zero pilots in the Southwest Pacific confronted aircraft of improved performance flown by increasingly skilled opponents whose numbers grew daily. One must also treat those Japanese pilots—battling against these tremendous odds—with a high degree of respect. In the New Guinea-Solomons campaign of 1942–1944, the victories came hard and were well earned on both sides.

This Zero Model 52c carries the victory markings of American insignia painted on its fuselage. The arrows show five single-engine confirmed kills, and the sixth is a probable. The two markings above the stars show a probable and a confirmed four-engine aircraft. Photographed in March 1945, fighter ace Naval Air Pilot 1/C Takeo Tanimizu of the 203rd Kokutai at Kagoshima recounts these victories.

Chapter 8

The End Draws Near–*Kamikaze* Attacks

The closing stages of the war resulted in successive defeats for the Japanese, yet the Zero remained essentially the same aircraft that had fought four years earlier. With increased demands placed upon it, urgent improvements were made in an attempt to at least *match* the opponent. The Zero's engine became more reliable and somewhat more powerful. Design changes improved its performance in some areas, and downgraded it in others due to added weight. An increase in weaponry gave it a bigger punch in striking power.

However, as the newer generation of Allied aircraft came on the scene, it became a losing battle, even though the Japanese pilots were just as courageous as in the early years of the Zero. For the young Japanese pilots who first flew the Zero, it was the modern weapon of the *samurai*, a nimble fighter not unlike the "slashing sword," with which Japan would defeat all its enemies. Now the situation was reversed and the Zero had become the *harakiri* blade, an instrument of sacrificial suicide, a one-way expendable weapon that carried its pilot to death and glory. Consequently, the Zero itself, once victorious in combat, was being expended in a tactical way that would otherwise bring certain defeat in fighter against fighter.

The story of *kamikaze* attacks is not new. Few may realize, however, that more Zeros were expended in these attacks than any other aircraft, including special craft designed for these suicide missions. Normally the older Zeros, such as the A6M2s, were fitted with a 550lb (250kg) bomb for these one-way missions. Initially, volunteer crews were limited to those having less flying experience and who stood little chance of survival in air-to-air combat or accurate dive-bombing, but who would be able to guide their aircraft in a final death dive upon an Allied ship. The few experienced pilots that remained often flew escort in the later model Zeros that had a better chance of survival while acting as escorts or decoys to draw the fire of the aggressive F6F Hellcat fighter screens and the veritable walls of antiaircraft which the US Fleet was able to set up.

The Battle of the Philippines, in October 1944, was the first major operation to employ these tactics on an organized basis. Several

In a kamikaze *attack, this Zero is attempting to crash into the battleship USS* Missouri, *off Okinawa. This unique photograph points out the relative sizes of these two opposing weapons, each deadly in its own way.* National Archives

American escort carriers were either sunk or severely damaged, as were other surface craft. Although these attacks were effective, they failed to prevent the US forces from landing on Luzon. Of the 331 Zeros launched in the Philippine operation in *kamikaze* attacks, 158 were able to reach their targets, destroying themselves in this desperate manner.

These tactics were used again during the invasion of Okinawa and other lesser locations throughout the ever-tightening web of combat around Japan. Only Japan's surrender prevented the implementation of a plan calling for the use of every Zero and comparable aircraft to be expended against the poised Allied invasion force in *kamikaze* attacks.

The philosophy of the *kamikaze* pilots had never been properly understood by Western minds, although many Allied pilots died in

With part of its tail shot away and a wing pierced by a shell, this A6M5 in a suicide dive upon the USS Essex *crashed out of control into the sea, instead.* National Archives

More Zeros were used in kamikaze *attacks than any other Japanese aircraft. Here is a Zero about to plunge into the hull of the American aircraft carrier USS* White Plains *in Leyte Gulf.* National Archives

Prepared for a heroic, yet somber mission are these A6M2-K trainers of the Genzan Kokutai. This picture, taken in the spring of 1945 at Kanoya Air Base on Kyushu, shows five of the two-seat Zeros poised for a planned kamikaze mission. Two A6M2s in their midst may serve as element leaders not committed to the final attack. Shoichi Tanaka

missions that were virtually suicidal. Anyone having flown numerous combat missions has at one time or other felt that his "number" was up on a particular mission, yet continued on after there was still time to turn back to safety. A vivid example is the story of US Navy Torpedo Squadron Eight at Midway. As each crew made its attack run, each was successively shot down prior to achieving its objective. Not only aviators demonstrated such bravery, but other combatants did as well. One of many examples was the case of the 20mm gun crews that manned their stations aboard the USS *Essex*, and who were enveloped in flames during their effort to beat off a *kamikaze* attack.

There was a fundamental philosophical difference between each side's interpretation of "heroism." The Japanese stoically accepted the situation because there was no hope for personal victory or escape from death. The Western mind, on the other hand, never would accept such a view. To the American, there had to be that last slim chance of survival; a feeling that, although many others around him may die, it was he who would somehow make it back.

The Japanese pilots who accepted and supported the suicide philosophy generally were those who held deep religious or patriotic convictions. These self-sacrificing attacks offered them a chance to attain various goals. The primary goal was to inflict losses on the enemy that might make them lose their overwhelming material advantage. Another motivation was to die bravely in the purest form of ancient Japanese tradition. Those who succeeded in returning from the normal combat encounters in which most of their comrades had been shot down were convinced that their survival was only temporary. A *kamikaze* mission afforded the opportunity to control one's destiny in the form of a devastating blow against the enemy for love of family and country.

These examples of self-sacrifice on such a scale have not been witnessed since the Pacific conflict. Combat situations since then have not fostered such extreme measures. And yet, the attraction to the hero figure remains; people still like to read about bravery and self-sacrifice. Perhaps it is a cyclical attribute; heroism may once again come into fashion, and then the bravery of the men who flew the Zero, particularly those who died in it, will become not only understandable, but admirable.

The desperate wartime situation for Japan in the closing months of the war caused many air units to commit themselves to kamikaze *attacks. Shown here prior to one of these attacks are Model 52c Zeros of the* Genzan Kokutai *at Kanoya Air Base, spring of 1945.* Shoichi Tanaka

Chapter 9

Evaluating the Zero

The war had been in progress for many months before any hands-on knowledge about the Zero could be established by the Western world. Most of what was available was obtained from pilots that had engaged the Zero in combat. Even line drawings showing the shape of the aircraft were misleading and highly inaccurate. It was essential that the Allies obtain an intact Zero at the earliest moment for close examination and flight evaluation.

That opportunity occurred during the Japanese diversionary attacks on Dutch Harbor in the Aleutian Islands during the Battle of Midway. On June 4, 1942, PO Tadayoshi Koga's A6M2 from the carrier *Ryujo* engaged in an attack, was hit by ground fire, and was forced to make a landing in a remote area of Akutan Island in the Aleutians. Landing with the gear down, the plane settled in the unexpected marsh surface and flipped on its back, killing the pilot. Little thought was given to retrieving this aircraft because of its inaccessibility—until a US Navy scouting party went to the crash site five weeks later and found the craft damaged, but repairable.

This Zero Model 21 was carefully removed and sent on a cargo vessel to the Assembly and Repair Department at NAS North Island, San Diego, arriving there in August 1942. In a secure area of the blimp hangar, the Zero was carefully inspected and repaired so that it could be flown for flight evaluation.

Major repairs were required for the tail, canopy, and nose. The broken Sumitomo propeller was probably replaced with an American-made Hamilton Standard, for both were reported to be identical. This task of repair without technical data to work from was difficult, yet it was completed by early October the same year.

In the meantime, this "Aleutian Zero" belonging to the US Navy began its evaluation in September 1942, for all the Allies to profit from. The test program was flown from NAS North Island at San Diego and, according to a letter from the flight test officer at NAS Anacostia (the "Japanese Nagoya Type Zero Fighter, Preliminary Test Report Of," dated October 31, 1942), it became the first formal American evaluation of the Zero.

Few arguments about the superiority of one aircraft over another can be resolved by comparing respective flight data charts and graphs with that of other aircraft because flight conditions are not always the same. Pilot skill is another factor. The best way to make general comparisons between two aircraft is to have both flown simultaneously with qualified test pilots.

In order to fairly evaluate the "Aleutian Zero," one of each type of US fighter was sent to San Diego for flight evaluation. Army Air Forces pilots from the AAF Proving Ground Group at Eglin Field, Florida, brought an example of the P-38F Lightning, P-39D-1 Airacobra, P-40F Warhawk, and the still very new P-51 Mustang. Navy pilots flew the F4F-4 Wildcat and an early model F4U-1 Corsair. From these tests came an intelligence summary of these findings, recorded in December 1942. Reprinted here in almost their entirety, they provide an excellent account of what the respective pilots would encounter when flying their aircraft against that of the enemy.

P-38F Lightning vs. Zero 21

To begin this test, both ships took off in formation on a prearranged signal. The Zero left the ground first and was about 300ft in the air before the P-38F was airborne. The Zero reached 5,000ft about 5sec ahead of the Lightning. From an indicated speed of 200mph (174kt), the Lightning accelerated away from the Zero in straight and level flight quite rapidly. The Zero was superior to the P-38 in maneuverability at speeds below 300mph (260kt).

The Japanese loss of this Zero on Akutan Island in the Aleutians, gave the Americans their first real chance to recover and examine the mysteries that surrounded the airplane. This Zero was part of the Japanese diversionary attack on Dutch Harbor in June 1942 from the carrier Ryujo. *National Archives*

The planes returned to formation at 5,000ft, then separated slightly as both ships reduced to their best respective climbing speed. Upon signal the climb was started to 10,000ft. Again the Zero was slightly superior in straight climbs, reaching 10,000ft about 4sec ahead of the P-38. Comparable accelerations and turns were tried with the same results.

From 10,000 to 15,000ft the two airplanes were about equal. Again comparable accelerations, speeds, and maneuverability were tried, with similar results as before.

In the climb from 15,000 to 20,000ft, the P-38 started gaining at about 18,200ft. At 20,000ft, the P-38 was superior to the Zero in all maneuvers except slow-speed turns. This advantage was maintained by the P-38 at all altitudes above 20,000ft.

One maneuver in which the P-38 was superior to the Zero was a high-speed reversal. It was impossible for the Zero to follow the P-38 in this maneuver at speeds above 300mph (260kt).

The test continued to 25,000 and 30,000ft. Due to the superior speed and climb of the P-38F at these altitudes, it could outmaneuver

In a closed-off portion of a hangar at NAS North Island, San Diego, the salvaged Zero is painstakingly repaired by the US Navy. The urgency for discovering the inner secrets of the enemy aircraft brought about the completion of this work in only three months. National Archives

US Navy ground crewmen prepare their captive for flight evaluation at San Diego. To avoid misidentification, the fighter was given a new paint finish of Navy blue-gray camouflage with standard US insignia. American Aviation Historical Society

the Zero by using these two advantages. The Zero was still superior in slow-speed turns.

P-39D-1 Airacobra vs. Zero 21

Takeoff was accomplished in formation on signal to initiate a climb from sea level to 5,000ft. The P-39D-1 was drawing 3000rpm and 70in manifold pressure on takeoff when the engine started to detonate, so manifold pressure was reduced to 52in. The Airacobra left the ground first and arrived at 5,000ft just as the Zero was passing 4,000ft. This manifold pressure of 52in could be maintained to 4,500ft just as the Zero was passing 4,000ft. At 5,000ft from a cruising speed of 230mph (200kt) indicated airspeed (IAS), the P-39 had a marked acceleration away from the Zero. Climb from 5,000 to 10,000ft at the respective best climbing speeds (thus eliminating zoom effect), the P-39

The Lockheed P-38F Lightning had superior speed and climb, but was no match for the Zero in a dog-fight.

reached 10,000ft approximately 6sec before the Zero. At 10,000ft, from a cruising speed of 220mph (191kt) IAS, the Airacobra still accelerated away from the Zero rapidly. Climbing from 10,000 to 15,000ft, both aircraft maintained equal rates of climb to 12,500ft. Above this altitude, the Zero walked away from the P-39.

In the climb from 15,000 to 20,000ft, the Zero took immediate advantage and left the Airacobra. The climb from 20,000 to 25,000ft was not completed since the P-39 was running low on fuel.

On a straight climb to altitude from take-off under the same conditions as before, the Airacobra maintained the advantage of the climb until reaching 14,800ft. Above this altitude the P-39 was left behind, reaching 25,000ft approximately 5min behind the Zero. At 25,000ft from a cruising speed of 180mph (156kt) IAS, the Zero accelerated away from the P-39 for three ship lengths. This lead was maintained by the Zero for one and a half minutes and it took the P-39D-1 another 30sec to gain a lead of one ship length.

An experienced Japanese pilot had already learned how to cope with the P-39. Their tactic was to begin a climb, just out of firing range of the P-39. At the point of stall for the P-39, the lighter weight Zero, which still had maneuvering air speed, would turn quickly toward the P-39 and attack while the Airacobra was defenseless without air speed. (Taken from an intelligence memorandum, "Japanese Fighter Plane Tactics," dated November 19, 1942.)

The North American P-51 Mustang had a diving advantage over that of the Zero, and generally was much faster. Although less maneuverable, the Mustang usually outclassed the Zero.

The Curtiss P-40F Warhawk was generally outclimbed by the Zero, which placed the P-40 at a disadvantage.

P-51 Mustang vs. Zero 21

The P-51 was drawing 3000rpm and 43in manifold pressure for its takeoff and climb to 5,000ft. The low manifold pressure was due to the setting on the automatic manifold pressure regulator. (This was the early Allison-powered Mustang.) The Zero left the ground and reached its best climb speed approximately 6sec before the P-51. It also reached 5,000ft approximately 6sec before the Mustang. However, the P-51 accelerated sharply away from the Zero at 5,000ft from a cruising speed of 250mph (217kt) IAS.

The climb from 5,000 to 10,000, and from 10,000 to 15,000ft produced the same results, having the Zero accelerate away from the P-51 in rate of climb. At 10,000ft from a cruising speed of 250mph (217kt) IAS, the Mustang again moved sharply away from the Zero, and at 15,000ft from a cruising speed of 240mph (208kt) IAS the P-51 had the advantage over the Zero, but slightly slower than at 5,000 and 10,000ft.

The P-51 could dive away from the Zero at any time. During this test, the P-51's powerplant failed to operate properly above 15,000ft, so the comparison was not continued above this altitude.

Japanese pilots had their tactics well planned. Mustang pilots accepted that head-on attacks became a game of "chicken." Should the Japanese pilot have an altitude advantage in this type of encounter, he would level off just out of firing range of both aircraft. At that point he would split-S and gener-

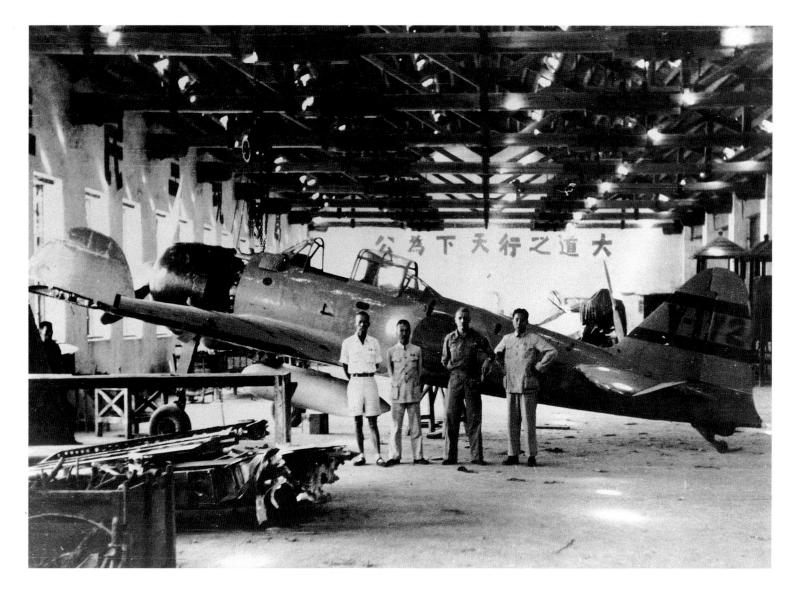

大道之行天下為公

The US Army was working hard to acquire a Zero for their own evaluation. This Zero found in China, formerly with the Tainan Kokutai, *was repaired by members of the 23rd Fighter Group based at Kweilin from August 1942. It was air ferried to Karachi, India, in February 1943 where it was shipped by boat to the United States.* USAF

ally end up on the tail of the Mustang pilot who often thought that the Zero was breaking off its attack. Should close-in maneuvering be the option selected by the Mustang pilot at this point of the encounter, the Japanese pilot immediately had the advantage because of the difference in maneuverability between the two fighters.

P-40F Warhawk vs. Zero 21

These tests were not completed with the P-40F because it was found impossible to obtain maximum engine operation.

A well-trained Japanese pilot in combat against the P-40 used the same climbing tactic as described for the P-39. Pursuing pilots often concentrated too heavily on their gunsight and would lose air speed without noticing. The Japanese pilot was then in charge with maneuvering air speed.

(*Note:* An interesting observation on the foregoing accounts are the engine problems mentioned in this report which included one aborted flight, yet no problems were indicated with the Zero. Also of interest are the acceleration comparisons at altitude that were started at optimum air speeds for the respective American fighters. The Zero, being the older design, performed admirably.)

F4F-4 Wildcat vs. Zero 21

The Zero was superior to the F4F-4 in speed and climb at all altitudes above 1,000ft, and was superior in service ceiling and range. Close to sea level, with the F4F-4 in neutral blower, the two planes were equal in level speed. In a dive, the two planes were equal

with the exception that the Zero's engine cut out in pushovers. There was no comparison between the turning circles of the two aircraft due to the relative wing loadings and resultant low stalling speed of the Zero. In view of the foregoing, the F4F-4 in combat with the Zero was basically dependent on mutual support, internal protection, and pull-outs or turns at high speeds where minimum radius is limited by structural or physiological effects of acceleration (expecting that the allowable acceleration on the F4F is greater than that of the Zero). However, advantage should be taken where possible of the superiority of the F4F in pushovers and rolls at high speed, or any combination of the two.

Japanese pilots soon learned of this defensive maneuver and had their own counter tactic. If the Zero pilot was making a beam attack or slightly from below or even level, he would fire a clearing shot and make a descending roll, usually to the left as if breaking off the attack. Expecting the Wildcat pilot to pursue the diving Zero, the Japanese pilot had already started a steep climb for another attack and rolling in on the Wildcat with advantage from above. (Taken from "Japanese Fighter Plane Tactics" memo, November 1942.)

F4U-1 Corsair vs. Zero 21

The Zero with its 950hp engine was by far inferior to the heavier 1,850hp F4U-1 in level and diving speeds at all altitudes. It fell short in climbs starting at sea level, and also above 20,000ft. Between 5,000 and 19,000ft the situation varied. With slightly more than the normal fighter load, which may be distributed to give equal range and gun power, the Zero was slightly superior in average maximum rate of climb. This superiority became negligible at altitudes where carburetor air temperatures in the F4U were down to normal; close to the blower shift points it was more noticeable. However, the Zero could not stay with the Corsair in high-speed climbs. The superiority of the F4U at 30,000ft was very evident, and would persist when carrying heavier loads.

In combat with the Zero, the Corsair could take full advantage of its speed along with its ability to push-over and roll at high speed if surprised. Due to its much higher wing loading, the F4U had to avoid any attempt to turn with the Zero unless at high speed, and could expect the latter to out-climb the Corsair at moderate altitudes and low air speeds. In this case, the F4U should be climbed at high air speed and on a heading that would open the distance and prevent the Zero from reaching a favorable position for diving attacks. After reaching 19,000 to 20,000ft, the Corsair had superior performance in climb and could choose its own position for attack.

During and after these comparison tests, this first of the Zeros to be captured and flown became an object of great curiosity. Charles A. Lindbergh is said to have been one of many noted airmen that were given a turn at flying this Zero. Several museums have since indicated that they have this aircraft in their collections, but the truth is that prior to a routine flight at NAS North Island, in the summer of 1944, the pilot of an SB2C Helldiver inadvertently taxied into the Zero and chopped it to pieces from the tail to the cockpit. The Zero was a total loss. All that remains are a few instruments and the port folding wing tip, which are on exhibit at the Navy Memorial Museum in the Washington Navy Yard.

In these and other evaluations, the Allies had discovered the Zero's weak points in diving speed, high-altitude performance, and maximum speed, all of which were sacrificed to obtain maneuverability and range, given the Zero's small engine. When the Allies started to use their well-planned tactics, it became much more difficult for the Zero to shoot down opposing aircraft. The best Allied tactic of all was "Do not attempt to dogfight against the Zero." Instead, Allied fighters, generally the Navy's Wildcats, operated in pairs and planned to be first in the attack when engaging the Zero. If the Zero tried to dogfight, each protected the other's rear by flying crisscross and not letting the Zero come from the rear. This was known as the "Thatch Weave." A climb for altitude often gave an advantage to later Allied fighters, allowing them to initiate another diving hit-and-run tactic against the Zero.

Japanese fighter tactics were often unique in themselves. Allied fighter pilots commented upon the Zero's ability to "make square turns," a frustrating maneuver that often placed the Zero being chased into firing position on the chaser. Japanese called this the *hineri-komi* maneuver. Developed around 1934, this maneuver roughly translates to "twisting-in." Perhaps this was the only original tactic developed by Japanese fighter pilots and seemingly not known to other fighter pilots of the world in the 1930s and 1940s. The maneuver consisted of a loop-the-loop, but executed with the aircraft at a slightly oblique angle to the straight-line direction of the loop, followed by a side-slipping maneuver while still in the loop. This caused the plane to "reef" sideways out of the loop, cutting down on turning radius considerably. In an attempt to stay with the Zero through such a maneuver, a pilot tends to place his airplane in the same attitude as the one being pursued, and with the heavier American aircraft, this approached impossibility in such a maneuver. This show of airmanship by well-seasoned JNAF pilots contributed much to establish the many myths about the Zero. (From a letter written by Osamu Tagaya, London, England, December 25, 1992.)

It might be worth pointing out that wartime attitudes in the United States make it appear as if development of tactics against the Zero was great cleverness on the part of the Allies. Obviously, it was of dire necessity and so development of effective anti-Zero tactics was a priceless advantage. However, this hides the fact that pre-war air combat doctrine in the United States, like the doctrine of all other major countries, was predicated on dogfighting techniques. Those were the rules by which aircraft engineers designed fighter air-

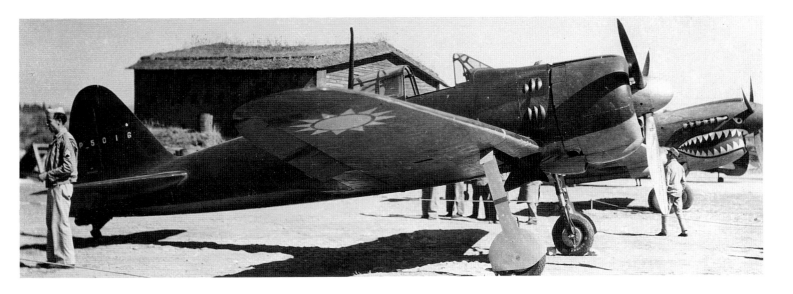

Since the accessory cowling was already missing when the Americans began preparing this Zero for flight, nonstandard louvered panels were fabricated *as replacements. At this early flying stage, Chinese markings were applied along with a Chinese serial number P-5016. USAF*

Curtiss test pilot H. Lloyd Child compared the Curtiss CW-21B to the Zero, primarily because of relative weights. The CW-21Bs flown in combat by the Netherlands East Indies forces, however, were no match for the Zero.

This Zero, captured in China, was severely damaged by heavy seas while aboard ship en route to the United States. The Curtiss-Wright Aircraft Company at Buffalo, New York, agreed to rebuild the aircraft so that it could be test-flown. Shown here, in October 1943, are test pilots and those associated with the project.

craft and to which service pilots were trained. When war came, it turned out that the Zero and the JNAF fighter pilots were so superior at the concept that the United States was *forced* to change the fighting rules in order to survive. Right to the end, this outstanding maneuverability was a superior quality that the Zero never relinquished.

At the time that the "Aleutian Zero" was reaching San Diego in August 1942 for repairs, the US Army came in possession of a Zero in China. The only way to retrieve this aircraft was to make it airworthy and fly it from Liuchow to the 23rd Fighter Group based at Kweilin. From there it was air ferried to Karachi, India, where it was shipped by boat to the United States. It was some time before repairs from damage caused during the boat shipment were completed at the Curtiss Airplane Factory at Buffalo, New York, but some

preliminary evaluation of the Zero's ability was made during the China-to-India ferry flight. The people at Curtiss completed the repairs on this Zero by mid-September 1943. There was no charge to the government for this rebuilding of the airplane, but as part of the agreement, the Curtiss test pilots were to be allowed to test fly the airplane before delivering it to the Army.

Within the realm of wartime test pilots, the name H. Lloyd Child of Curtiss is among the better known. His report about the airplane had some interesting comments. Contrary to earlier statements by the Japanese involved with the Zero in that the control between the three axis was "balanced and better than the foreign aircraft evaluated," Child thought that "the coordination between the air controls was poor. This is especially noticeable between the light rudder control and the

heavy aileron controls." Child also commented that he did not feel that this aircraft would accelerate like a P-36 in a dogfight. He would prefer a Curtiss P-36 or a P-40 or a "St. Louis Model 21" [Curtiss CW-21] to the Japanese Zero in a fight. While his comment could have been valid, he also noted that the propeller pitch limits were out of adjustment, a factor that would adversely affect the true potential of the airplane. His concluding remark came as a surprise: "A commercial version of it [the Zero] would appeal to a sportsman pilot after the war. Its clean lines, simplicity, lightness and ease of handling for the private owner would make this a desirable airplane for a millionaire private owner. We [Curtiss] should keep it in mind in the event that we develop the Model SNC-1 airplane later for this market." The Model 21 was a light-weight export fighter by Curtiss-Wright, and the SNC-1 was

The captured A6M2, when outfitted in US markings of 1943 vintage. After flight evaluations at Eglin Field, Florida, and suffering from continual mechanical problems, the airplane was relegated to bond drive showings and eventually was scrapped. USAF

From the parts of five Model 32s, American and Australian technicians assembled one flyable example of this new Zero model at Eagle Farm Airport, Brisbane. M. P. Clark

When Allied forces moved on to Buna airstrip on New Guinea in late 1942, they were able to examine what was thought to be a new Japanese fighter. This was the A6M3 Model 32, a clipped-wing version of the standard Zero. It had a new engine with approximately 150 more horsepower. The "Q" designator painted on the tail was used briefly by the 582nd Kokutai. USAF

a tandem Navy trainer version of this airplane. (From a Curtiss Airplane Company memorandum dated September 20, 1943, titled "Flight Test Report—Japanese Zero.")

After six months of strenuous work at rebuilding this "China Zero" (Mitsubishi s/n 3372) it was turned over to the Army at Wright Field for their evaluation. This allowed the Army to have their own Zero for evaluation, since reports indicated that there was feeling that all the facts that would be useful

about the Zero were not made available by the US Navy. As a result of its own testing, the Army prepared observations to be disseminated to its pilots. The Army's conclusions were similar to the Navy's. (Based on Informational Intelligence Summary No. 85, US Army Air Forces, titled "Flight Characteristics of the Japanese Zero Fighter," dated December 1942.)

Army analysis stressed the warning to avoid dogfighting with the Zero at a speed less than 300mph (260kt) IAS. In developing tactics against the Zero, pilots were reminded that the Zero had a disadvantage of a slower rate of roll at high speeds and that the rate of roll was faster from right to left than from left to right. According to Saburo Sakai, he favored the *hineri-komi* loop to the left when given the choice. It became well known that the Zero's engine cut out under negative load conditions. However, the report continues,

"the engine performance of the Zero is superior to the present service type engines without turbo superchargers. This superiority is recognized in the fact that maximum manifold pressure can be maintained from sea level to 16,000ft." (Adjustments to the engine and propeller must have been made to correct discrepancies noted in Lloyd Child's report on this particular Zero, which were quite the contrary.)

All of the foregoing comparisons were based upon the early model of the Zero. As Allied aircraft improved, the Japanese made advancements in their fighter technology. Although new Japanese designs were in the offing, their development was painstakingly slow, and it was the Zero that had to remain in the forefront during the war from start to finish.

When the Allies met later models of the Zero, they needed examples with which to

While at Brisbane, preliminary flight evaluation was made with this rebuilt Zero Model 32. It could out-climb American types at that time, but was slower in level flight. M. P. Clark

When US Marines went ashore on Saipan in June 1944, a number of Japanese airplanes were captured intact before the island was fully secured.

Among them were examples of the latest model Zero, the A6M5, and many spare engines for the aircraft.

Twelve A6M5 Zeros on Saipan were gathered and shipped to the United States for evaluation. The Zero on exhibit in the National Air and Space Museum, Washington, D.C., was captured within this group on Saipan and carries the markings of the 261st Kokutai. National Archives

make firsthand evaluations. Examples of the Zero Model 32, initially code named Hamp, were first found at Buna airstrip in New Guinea by Australian and US forces in late December 1942. Painstakingly, several were disassembled, moved through backwoods roads and jungle undergrowth to the shore where they were transported by barge to Australia. It was at Eagle Farm Airport at Brisbane that an Allied intelligence unit rebuilt, among other types, a Hamp for evaluation. When this example was completed, it was test flown in Australia before being sent to Wright Field, Ohio, for further evaluation.

Pilots who had flown the earlier Zero 21 reported that the Model 32 had improved rate of roll, which they attributed to the shortened wings. Although heavier by about 280lb, the Hamp did have an increase in speed due to the shortened wings and the more powerful engine turning a larger propeller. However, the performance of this new model was not all that superior to that of the earlier type. In ad-

dition, because of the combined effect of a smaller fuel tank and an engine that consumed fuel at a higher rate, the Model 32's range was reduced when compared to the Zero 21's. This was important information, for superiority in range was a critical advantage for Japanese aircraft. As the Japanese were forced to retreat from island to island, they still had to reach out and defend Japanese air space.

A flight report was made about this airplane. The conclusion states: "The airplane is highly maneuverable. Its rate of climb at rated power is high as compared with the rate of climb of AAF fighter aircraft at rated power. However, its speed is slow, it does not contain any armor protection for the pilot, it is not equipped with self sealing fuel tanks and its armament is light." (Engineering Division Memorandum, Report Serial Number ENG 47-1726-A, "Performance Flight Test of a Japanese Hamp, AAF No. EB-201," March 28, 1944.)

When the JNAF introduced yet a newer model into the Pacific war, the Model 52, they hoped to again achieve the upper hand. However, this would not happen because at the same time, the US Navy introduced the Grumman F6F Hellcat, striking a close balance. When the new Zero was engaged in combat, it demonstrated aspects in its performance that differed from the previous models. A firsthand evaluation was again necessary.

It was not until the occupation of Saipan, as Allied forces moved into the Marianas, that Model 52s were captured. Twelve examples were captured and shipped to the United States in July 1944 for evaluation. Off-loaded at San Diego, at least two of these examples, after being checked, were flown to NAS Anacostia where the Technical Air Intelligence Center was then located. After further work, at least one was flown to NAS Patuxent River, Maryland, where comparison flight tests were made with Allied aircraft. When the observations that follow were formalized, reports of these comparisons were forwarded to units in the Pacific that were encountering the new Zero. Here are those findings. (Air Command Weekly Intelligence Summary, Allied Technical Air Intelligence Unit, South East Asia, "Flight Trials of Zeke 52," December 17, 1943.)

F4U-1D Corsair vs. Zero 52

Tested against this Zero 52 was the latest model of the Corsair, the F4U-1D. This differed from the earlier Corsair evaluated against the Zero 21 by having a water-injection engine, giving it improved performance. Both aircraft were flown side by side, making all things equal at the beginning of the flight comparison test. In a race for altitude, the best

One of the A6M5s captured on Saipan and brought to this country now flies with the Planes of Fame Museum in California. It carries the markings of the 261st Kokutai, to which it was last assigned before capture. Planes of Fame

The Planes of Fame A6M5 shown in formation with a Grumman F6F Hellcat. Plane of Fame

climb of the F4U-1D was equal to the Zero's up to 10,000ft, about 750fpm (feet per minute) better at 18,000ft, and about 500fpm better at 22,000ft and above. Best climb speeds of the Corsair and Zero were 156mph (135kt) and 122mph (105kt) IAS, respectively.

The F4U-1D was faster than the Zero 52 at all altitudes, having the least margin of 42mph (37.5kt) at 5,000ft and the widest difference of 80mph (70kt) at 25,000ft. Top speeds attained were 413mph (360kt) true air speed (TAS) at 20,400ft for the Corsair and 335mph (290kt) TAS at 18,000ft for the Zero.

Rate of roll for the Zero was equal to that of the Corsair at speeds under 230mph (200kt) and inferior above that speed due to high control forces in the Zero. Maneuverability of the Zero was remarkable at speeds below 202mph (175kt), being far superior to that of the Corsair. In slow-speed turns the Zero could gain one turn in three and a half at 10,000ft. At speeds around 202mph (175kt), however, by using flaps the F4U could stay with the Zero for about one-half turn, or until its speed fell off to 173mph (150kt).

Initial dive accelerations of the Zero and the Corsair were about the same, after which the Corsair was far superior, and slightly superior in zooms after dives.

F6F-5 Hellcat vs. Zero 52

The Zero climbed about 600fpm better than the F6F up to 9,000ft, after which the advantage fell off gradually until the two aircraft were about equal at 14,000ft. Above this altitude the Hellcat had the advantage, varying from 500fpm better at 22,000ft, to about 250fpm better at 30,000ft. Best climb speeds of the F6F-5 and Zero 52 were 150mph (130kt) and 122mph (105kt) IAS, respectively.

The F6F-5 was faster than the Zero 52 at all altitudes, having the least margin of 25mph (21.5kt) at 5,000ft and the widest difference of 75mph (65kt) at 25,000ft. Top speeds attained were 409mph (355kt) at 21,600ft for the Hellcat, and 335mph (290kt) at 18,000ft for the Zero.

Comments on rate of roll, dive, maneuverability, and turns for the Hellcat were identical to those made on the Corsair, except the attempts at turning with flaps were not mentioned.

FM-2 Wildcat vs. Zero 52

The FM-2 was a General Motors-built Wildcat having a 1,350hp engine replacing the 1,200hp engine on the earlier F4F-4. In climbs, the Zero was about 400fpm less than that of the Wildcat starting at sea level, becoming equal at 4,000ft, and 400fpm better at 8,000ft.

The Grumman F6F-5 Hellcat was faster than the Zero 52 at all altitudes. When encountering the Zero at higher speeds, the Hellcat had the advantage. NASM

Climbs became equal again passing 13,000ft, and the Zero was only slightly inferior above 13,000ft. Best climb speeds of the FM-2 and Zero were 138mph (120kt) and 122mph (105kt) IAS, respectively.

The FM-2 was 6mph (5kt) faster than the Zero at sea level, becoming 4mph (3.5kt) slower at 5,000ft and dropping to 26mph (22.5kt) slower at 30,000ft. Top speeds attained were 321mph (288kt) TAS at 13,000ft for the FM-2, and 335mph (290kt) at 18,000ft for the Zero. Rate of roll of the two fighters was equal at 184mph (160kt) and under. The Zero became inferior at higher speeds due to heavy stick forces. Turns of the FM-2 and Zero were very similar, with a slight advantage in favor of the Zero 52. The Zero could gain one turn in eight at 10,000ft.

The Zero was slightly superior to the FM-2 in initial dive acceleration, after which the dives were about the same. Zooms after dives were about equal for the two aircraft.

Air Tactics

The results of these evaluations concluded that with all three American aircraft, it was best not to engage the Zero in a dogfight, and not to follow it in a loop or half-roll with pull-through (split-S). When attacking, the superior power and speed of the Hellcat and Corsair were to be used for engaging the Zero at the most favorable moment. For the Wildcat, any altitude advantage possible was to be maintained. In all three cases, to evade a Zero, the best method was to roll and dive away in a high-speed turn.

From this American report describing the performance of the later model Zero and how to cope with it, the point was obvious that the aircraft was still a serious threat in any air battle. The weakest aspect of the Zero at this stage of its operational life was the lack of skilled pilots to fly them. It can be safely assumed that the American pilots flying the Zero for these tests were far more qualified through experience and training than the Japanese pilots normally encountered in combat.

In the final analysis, the Zero could never fully be discounted as a lethal fighting machine, even toward the end of the war. Although the Zero was inferior in some respects to the later Allied fighters, much of the air battle depended upon the skill of the respective pilots and their wise use of air tactics. The two warring navies of the Pacific war were quite similar in the first six months of the war. The margin of victory in air battles was very thin. One Japanese air historian described the situation being like two sumo wrestlers of equal skill and strength tussling in the ring. One side was able to exert a mere fraction more pressure than the other. The twitch of a muscle at the precise moment may cause his opponent to teeter and fall out of the ring. An air victory was often that close, and the victor was much more magnificent for it.

Unlike the Confederate Air Force Zero, the Planes of Fame Zero is still flown with its Sakae engine. Planes of Fame

Chapter 10

The Zero Matures

When the Zero first entered combat, its role was that of an aggressor. As the war continued, the Zero took on a different role—that of defending itself against a more aggressive enemy with improved weaponry. In an attempt to stay abreast with a rapidly changing wartime situation, frequent modifications had to be made to the Zero. Yet, only so much "stretch" can be applied to one basic design. After a certain point, an entirely new design must be made that will make the best use of the latest technologies.

In the case of the Zero, the JNAF failed to introduce a substantially improved replacement for it, to match the speed, armament, and protection of the modern Allied fighters that began arriving in the Pacific in late 1942. Consequently, the Zero faced an even more potent enemy having both quality and quanti-

ty in its aircraft, while the Japanese pilots were left to rely on an array of improvements made to the Zero's basic 1937 design specifications. Its obsolescence could no longer be shielded through modifications after 1943. Yet, by necessity, it was kept in production until the surrender of Japan, and the Japanese built more Zeros than they did any other aircraft.

The Zero ran the gamut over its life span, from the superiority it enjoyed over China and the Pacific during the first year of the war, to the inferiority it endured during the final desperate attempts to ward off swarms of Allied carrier-based aircraft and B-29s over the home islands of Japan. By examining the modifications made to the Zero over its long life, and the reasons for these design changes, we encapsulate the history of the Zero, and in a way, summarize the Pacific war itself.

The JNAF's project designators, or short titles, head the following descriptions of the various models of the Zero Fighter. In the short title system, the first letter identified the aircraft mission. For the A6M5, the *A* stood for *carrier-based fighter*; the 6 meant that the design was the sixth in the category of carrier-based fighters; the *M* was for *Mitsubishi*, the designing firm; and the last number identified a major variation.

Also included is the long title for each Zero model. The JNAF simultaneously used this identifier as well, in documents and on nameplates attached to airframes. For convenience, Japanese users often abbreviated the long titles, cutting them down to just a few characters. A long title such as Type Zero Carrier-Based Fighter Model 52 (*Rei Shiko Kanjo Sentoki Go Ni Gata*) became Zero Fighter

Zero Model 21, A6M2. Folding wing tips were the most noticeable feature of this model. The aileron balancing tabs identify this example as a Nakajima-built A6M2. This is one of the group of Zeros captured on Saipan. USAF

Zero Model 11, A6M2. This first of the production models did not have folding wing tips and was initially used as a land-based interceptor. It was the lightest of all production Zero models, with a net weight of about 3,676lb and a maximum over-loaded weight of about 6,146lb. R. Seely

Model 52 (Rei Sentoki Go Ni Gata), or simply Zero Fighter (Reisen). In the West, Zero 52 is the most succinct abbreviation of the long title given above—or Zeke 52, when using the Allied code name.

In the two-digit model number—Model 52, for instance—that fell at the end of a long title, the first digit signified airframe variations and the second represented engine variations. As such, the more correct way of reading the numbers is five-two, meaning the fifth airframe design variation and the second type or model of engine.

Before this two-digit identification system was put into use over a two-year period beginning in mid-1941, the JNAF had a mark-number/model-number system of identifying variations. The mark number showed major design variations (airframe, engine, or even manufacturer) and the model number showed significant modifications. The Navy made this change in nomenclature to more aptly identify various types and models, not for security reasons. But it had the effect of

confusing the Allies during the first couple of years of the war because of airplanes like the Zero seeming to have two different designations. At one time, these two names for the Zero made Allied intelligence think that the designations showed that both the JAAF and the JNAF used the Zero, when in fact, the JAAF did not fly Zeros.

A6M1

When the Imperial Japanese Navy accepted the 12-Experimental Carrier-Based Fighter (12 Shisaku Seizo Kanjo Sentoki) on September 14, 1939, it received the designation A6M1 retroactively. This short title applied only to the first two aircraft in the A6M series. Each was powered by the 875hp Mitsubishi Zuisei 13 engine and was unique in plan form and profile to those that followed: overall length was about 28ft 10in (8.79m), and the vertical tail was broad.

The Zuisei engine had a down-draft carburetor, making an air scoop at the top of the cowling a necessity. Artists usually show the air scoop as a 90-degree elbow-shaped pipe awkwardly protruding from the accessory section into the airstream atop the engine cowling. But no photos have been found to show that this concept is correct. Contradictory evidence in the form of A6M1 parts drawings that appear in early technical manuals indicate that the air scoop was under the engine cowling in a manner similar to that of Mitsubishi's early version of the F1M2 observation biplane, Pete, which was powered by this same engine.

A6M2

The third A6M prototype was powered by the more powerful 950hp Nakajima Sakae 12 engine. The fuselage was lengthened nearly 11in, partly due to moving the vertical tail farther aft, about 13.8in at the rudder hinge line.

This gave the tail narrower base, producing for the first time the familiar Zero profile. The horizontal tail span was increased by about 4in and was raised 7.4in from its former position on the fuselage centerline. Ailerons were given more surface area by moving their roots inboard by one wing station, which in turn reduced the landing flap length.

The new engine brought with it an updraft carburetor, which called for relocation of the air scoop. The designers put the scoop at the bottom of the engine cowling, routing it above the oil-cooler air scoop and cutting it short so that it was similar to the oil cooler housing in length. The shape was changed after the sixth airframe, whereupon a smaller and better shaped oil-cooler scoop appeared for the first time, along with a repositioned oil cooler. The designers also brought the carbu-

retor scoop forward to the bottom lip of the engine cowling.

Early A6M2s were known by their experimental name until the design was accepted by the JNAF on July 31, 1940, whereupon the long service title became Type Zero Mk. 1 Carrier-Based Fighter Model 1 *(Rei Shiki Ichi Go Kanjo Sentoki Ichi Gata)*. The Navy applied the service name retroactively to all A6M2s. Later, when the new designation system came into effect, the airplane became the Type Zero Carrier-Based Fighter Model 11 *(Rei Shiki Kanjo Sentoki Ichi Ichi Gata)*, the translation most recognized in the English-speaking world.

Of the 64 Zero Model 11s, only three were actually outfitted to be tested for the role of carrier fighter: numbers 6, 27, and 28. The rest were operated as interceptor fighters, and many served in China, where actual combat

Zero Model 32, A6M3. Squared wing tips, a new and longer engine, and a sleek cowl with the carburetor air scoop built into its upper half are the iden- *tifying features of this model that was once code named Hamp. USAF*

conditions pointed out certain shortcomings requiring modification or redesign. The needed changes, combined with some identified by the manufacturer, were made as soon as remedies could be found. Included were redesign of the antenna mast and fittings, improvement of the landing gear up-lock mechanism and bearing points, and redesign of the tail wheel shock strut. From the 47th airframe, the aft end of the canopy was given a detachable section in order to ease disassembly of the fuselage, and the camera-gun mounting fixtures were moved from the left wing to the right.

With the sixth airframe came the first attempt to reduce the 39.36ft (12m) wingspan to a more manageable size for carrier operations. The existing size barely cleared the elevator shaft openings of the carrier deck elevators, which made wing-tip damage highly possible. Mitsubishi designer Jiro Horikoshi names Hirotsugu Hirayama as the man who designed the wing-tip folding mechanism to temporarily reduce this overall wingspan. If that is so, then Hirayama had one false start when he came up with the design that required the tip to be pulled out slightly on tubular hinges and then folded *under* the wing. A simpler design was tried on the No. 27 A6M that consisted mainly of smaller latches and hinges. The tip of about 20in (500mm) folded up to reduce the

Zero Model 22, A6M3. The wing form of the Model 21 (without the foldable tips) and the engine and cowling of the Model 32 identify this aircraft as a Model 22. Shoichi Tanaka

Zero Model 52, A6M5. The carburetor air scoop retained in the upper cowling, individual exhaust stacks, and a shorter wing with nonfolding round tips are the best identifying features of this model.

overall span to 35.93ft (10.955m), and it became standard from airframe No. 67 to the end of A6M2 production. Had the entire wing been made to fold to save deck space like that of the Wildcat, Hellcat, and others of the US Navy, it would have increased the weight of the structure, a penalty that the Japanese did not want to pay. The Navy gave to these later models the new nomenclature of Type Zero Mk.1 Carrier-Based Fighter Model 2 *(Rei Shiki Ichi Go Kanjo Sentoki Ni Gata)*. Later, under the revised system, the name became Type Zero Carrier-Based Fighter Model 21 *(Rei Shiki Kanjo Sentoki Ni Ichi Gata)*.

Horikoshi states that the short title was given a suffix to differentiate between the Zero Model 11 and the Model 21, the former becoming A6M2a and the latter becoming A6M2b. It is likely that these designations were after-the-fact book terms only. No such short titles were ever found on the nameplates of Zero Model 21s that Allied intelligence examined.

By the 327th A6M, which came out of the factory during September 1941, no further modifications were needed. The problems with aileron flutter and balancing trim tabs, as previously described, had seemingly been resolved. The Navy was well pleased with their new fighter. There was a need for greater Zero production, so the Navy issued production contracts to Nakajima, starting in November 1941. The Nakajima-built Zero 21, which out-numbered the Mitsubishi-built fighter, became the workhorse of the JNAF during the first two years of the Pacific war. But this fighter revealed certain shortcomings both to its users and to its opponents. Change was imperative: either a new type of naval fighter or a new Zero model was desperately needed and right away!

A6M3

The need to improve the high-altitude and climb performance of the Zero had been recognized by 1941. Under the terms of a project designated A6M3, Mitsubishi designers modified two airframes in May and June 1941, and equipped both with the new Sakae 21 engine. This upgraded engine had a two-speed, two-stage supercharger, down-draft carburetor, and revised propeller gearing that permitted a 10ft propeller instead of the 9ft 6in propeller used on the A6M2.

The new engine was rated at 1,130hp for takeoff. Although the engine diameter was the same as the Sakae 12, it weighed more and was longer. Fitting the new engine in the Zero's airframe required moving the firewall back 8in and designing a new cowling. Openings for the nose-mounted machine guns were placed in the front of the cowling, replacing the earlier gun troughs positioned along the top of the cowling.

Flight tests of the prototype A6M3 began in the summer of 1941. Unfortunately, a substantial performance increase did not materialize. The gain in speed was a mere 5.5kt. Pilots flying the test models recommended removing the folding wing tips entirely. This was perhaps tried for the first time on the third A6M3 prototype, which appeared in January 1942.

The modification of eliminating the folding tips and fairing over the blunt end reduced not only the wingspan, but also the aileron length by about 1ft. The engineers did this by eliminating the outer 4in and terminating the inner end by one wing station farther outboard from that of the A6M2. These changes improved the rate of roll and reduced stick forces for the pilot. Level speed was also improved.

Because of these improvements, the Navy shelved production plans for the full-span A6M3, and instead ordered the shortened span version to be put into production in the spring of 1942. The Navy assigned this new model a temporary designation under the old system, calling it the Type Zero Mk.2 Carrier-Based Fighter *(Rei Shiki Ni Go Kanjo Sentoki)*, principally because officials had not yet decided what name would be right for this new model under the new system.

When the clipped-wing Zero was first seen by the Allies in August 1942, at airfields in New Guinea and the Solomon Islands, it was thought to be a new Japanese fighter. It was given the Allied code name Hap in honor of Gen. Henry H. "Hap" Arnold of the Air

The Zero Model 52 (A6M5). Rikyu Watanabe

Zero Model 52a, A6M5a. This submodel had increased cannon ammunition, achieved by changing from a drum-fed to a belt-fed cannon, which eliminated the tear-drop bulges on the underside of the wings. Later examples had thicker wing skin, permitting a higher diving speed. T. Kanamura

Force. But when Arnold found out about the name, he was reported to be less than flattered, and it was recoded Hamp. When Americans had their first close look at this model in New Guinea in late 1942, they became aware that it was a modification of the basic Zero. The Allied code name prevailed until May 1944, when captured documents revealed that the Japanese had adopted this model on January 29, 1943, as the Type Zero Carrier-Based Fighter Model 32 (*Rei Shiki Kanjo Sentoki San Ni Gata*), whereupon the Allies revised their code name to Zeke 32.

The JNAF operated the Zero 32 over New Guinea and the Solomon Islands beginning in August 1942. But the model was not an overwhelming success. The reduction in wing area by just over 9sq-ft and the shorter ailerons improved roll and speed, but the combined changes with the new engine added 280lb to the aircraft. About 40lb of this added weight came from new 100-round magazines for the two-wing cannons, an increase of 40 rounds

per gun. Fuel quantity had to be reduced by about 22gal to accommodate the longer engine and avoid changing the overall length of the airplane. The tactical combat radius suffered from this change and the added thirst of the Sakae 21 engine.

On August 7, 1942, the US 1st Marine Division landed on Guadalcanal, making apparent to the Japanese defenders an immediate need for an extended range fighter. Zero 32s had just arrived at Rabaul, but were too limited in range for the long missions to Guadalcanal. Instead, the older A6M2s were used for these missions.

Air commanders communicated their need to naval headquarters and in turn to Mitsubishi. Designers restored the full span and added a small fuel tank, holding about 12gal, in each outer wing section. The old idea of the aileron balancing tab, which had been tried unsuccessfully on the A6M2, was reinstated to reduce control forces on the once-again larger aileron. Desperate for better fighters, the JNAF approved the changes in November and the first production versions came off the assembly lines in December 1942. These long-wing A6M3s were known as the Model 22.

The reversal in model number, from 32 back to 22, resulted from restoration of the rounded wing tips that matched the airframe of the Zero Model 21, yet retained the more

powerful but fuel-hungry Sakae 21. Even so, the additional 24gal gave the Model 22 the longest range of them all, about 100 miles more than that of the astonishing Model 21.

Engineers made two more modifications to the Model 22 before production ceased in August 1943. One was the addition of a cockpit-controlled rudder trim tab; the other, the introduction of the long-barrel Type 99 Mk. 2 Model 3 cannon. Planes with this latter modification came to be known as the Model 22a in administrative references.

A6M4

The assignment of this designation to a Zero model has been in question for a long time, since no authoritative records have ever been found to prove its use. The designation may have been set aside for a proposed model that never materialized. Some think that it was associated with an A6M3 that was to be equipped with a turbo-supercharged engine, as suggested in 1968 by the Zero's designer, Jiro Horikoshi. But the reason is not really known.

A6M5

Although something of an improvement, the Zero 22 suffered heavy losses during the desperate defense of Rabaul in 1943. JNAF hopes that a new interceptor fighter—the J2M

Zero Model 52c, A6M5c. External feature was the addition of a second wing gun outboard of the cannon and rocket rails under the wing.

(Jack)—would help regain air superiority in 1943 were dashed when development and production lagged. Again it became necessary to modify the existing Zero in an attempt to simplify and speed up production and to increase the diving speed. Once again, engineers redesigned the wing, this time changing the squared-off wing tips to fixed rounded tips. The wing-tip folding mechanisms which were merely faired over in the squared-off version. The modified wing had about the same span as the Zero 32's wing coupled with the increased fuel capacity of the Zero 22's. A test airframe of the Model 22 Modified, identified by its shorter wing was in hand by June 1943, which served as a prototype for this variant, the A6M5.

The Mitsubishi company probably undertook limited production of the Model 22 with the shortened wings before settling upon the final form of the A6M5. In arriving at this new model, the Model 22 had the collector ring and two exhaust ports of the Model 32. This eventually gave way to individual exhaust stacks on its Sakai 21 engine which is the identifying feature of the A6M5 Model 52. This change directed the high velocity exhaust gas backward for additional thrust.

No statistics can be found to tell how many of these short-wing Model 22 airframes might have been turned out. It is quite likely that less than 50 were produced. However many there were, these M3-M5 hybrids served as prototypes for the A6M5 and may be regarded as an intermediate design. Mitsubishi

produced them near the end of the production run of Model 22, which totaled 560. News of this intermediate design could make some enthusiasts begin to wonder if the A6M4 designation might have been set aside for this variation and then quickly dropped in favor of the true A6M5 with individual exhaust stacks.

The true A6M5, Type Zero Carrier-Based Fighter Model 52 (*Rei Shiki Kanjo Sentoki Go Ni Gata*), came along in August 1943, as production changed from the Model 22. The JNAF adopted it as a standard service type on August 23. Captured documents show that the true first production A6M5 had serial number (s/n) 3904 and differed from the A6M3 Model 22 in the following ways:

- Wing tips were rounded and shortened about 19.69in (500mm).
- Ailerons were on the outer side of wing station 12 and their outer ends were narrowed and tapered to blend into the wing-tip curve. The balancing tabs and their linkage to the landing flaps were abolished, and ground-adjustable fixed tabs were substituted.
- The landing flaps extended to wing station 12.
- The collector exhaust pipe system was abolished and individual stacks substituted. Accompanying this change, the cowl flaps were notched.
- The dive-bombing speed limit was increased to 360kt IAS as a result of the wing tips being shortened.
- An increase in net weight of about 22lb (10kg).
- An increase in maximum speed of 2–13kt.

The unknown number of modified Model 22s and the new Model 52s were pressed into service in September or October of 1943,

which coincided with the initial appearance of the new F6F Hellcat. When faced with the heavier armament of the F6F, the new Zeros were just too lightly constructed and still had inadequate protection for pilot and fuel.

The first 370 Model 52s had no fire-fighting devices of any kind. But to try to increase survivability, Mitsubishi began installing an automatic CO_2 fire extinguisher system with the 371st airframe. This system protected the four wing fuel tanks.

A6M5a

(*Note:* The use of *a*, *b*, and *c* in the A6M5 designation is for translation conveniences. In actual Japanese usage, these were *Ko, Otsu, and Hei.*)

After Mitsubishi built 747 Zero 52s, Navy and company engineers came together for yet another improvement. These new modifications were to be associated with the first of three submodels within the A6M5 series.

The Model 52a changes involved installation of the manually charged Type 99 Mk.2 Model 4 belt-fed Oerlikon cannon in place of the drum-fed model. This new cannon modification had an experimental feed block attached to it, one designed by the Air Technical Arsenal. The gain in ammunition was about 25 rounds per gun, but at the price of a net-weight increase of about 6.6lb (3kg).

In that form, Mitsubishi built 114 A6M5a airframes before the company won approval to use a feed block of their own design and to combine their design with thicker outer wing panels for an increase in maximum diving speed to 400kt. The thicker wing skin panels made the new weight go up by about 33lb (15kg) and the maximum level speed down by about 3kt compared to the original Model 52.

Mitsubishi built 277 of the A6M5a airframes equipped with their feed-block design before the next major modifications, for a total of 391.

A6M5b

Engineers sought a measure of protection for the Zero pilot by placing a 1.75in (45mm) panel of bullet-resistant glass behind the windshield. To increase firepower, one of the two fuselage-mounted 7.7mm machine guns was replaced by a 13mm machine gun, resulting in the first change in armament size since the first prototype of the Zero. These were the A6M5b, of which 470 were built.

A three-view drawing of the Model 52c (A6M5c). The A6M5c was fitted with a 13mm machine gun mounted outboard of the 20mm cannon on each wing. The diagonal camouflage paint separation line on the fuselage side marks this as a Nakajima-built Zero. Rikyu Watanabe

A6M5c

Every attempt was being made to maintain the fighting effectiveness of the Zero, which everyone now realized was destined to carry the fight without a replacement. The next improvements brought the A6M5c into production. The emphasis was on increased firepower and pilot protection.

Firepower was increased by adding two Type 3 13mm machine guns to the wing armament. These two guns, one for each side, were placed outboard of the two 20mm cannons. This finally stretched the design over the limit of its ability to carry guns, ammunition, bombs, and fuel and still show a credible performance. To get the weight back into acceptable limits, the designers removed the remaining 7.7mm machine gun from the fuselage. The final armament was then three 13mm machine guns and two 20mm cannons. Added to

this were provisions for carrying small air-to-air rocket bombs on under-wing racks.

Defensive additions were also attended to. For the first time on production lines, armor plate was installed behind the pilot's seat, and several panels of bullet-resistant glass were mounted on a frame behind the pilot's head.

To keep the aircraft's center of gravity within limits, the fuel load was redistributed and reduced. A 37gal self-sealing tank was installed behind the pilot at mid-fuselage. The main wing tanks were reduced to 41gal each and the two small outer wing tanks were reduced to 6.5gal each. The droppable auxiliary tank was reduced to 79gal. The total fuel carried then became 227gal. All of these changes increased the net weight of the Model 52c by about 600lb over that of the Model 52. The maximum speed went down accordingly—by about 13kt.

By now, Zero designer Jiro Horikoshi had moved on to the urgent project of designing the A7M Reppu, Allied code name Sam, as Mitsubishi's replacement for the Zero. The job of further modifying the Zero was left to design engineer Eitaro Sano, who could readily see that, with the vast increases in weight, the performance of the A6M5c would be greatly impaired if the Sakae 21 engine had to be retained. His team's proposal to the BuAir was to incorporate Mitsubishi's own engine of greater horsepower into the Zero. The new engine was the 1,350hp Kinsei 62 engine, which would provide an increase of 250hp. With this engine, the design staff felt that the Zero might well be restored to performance equal to that of the F6F Hellcat.

To the grave disappointment of the designers, the Navy refused to release any of the larger engines. Most were already committed as an

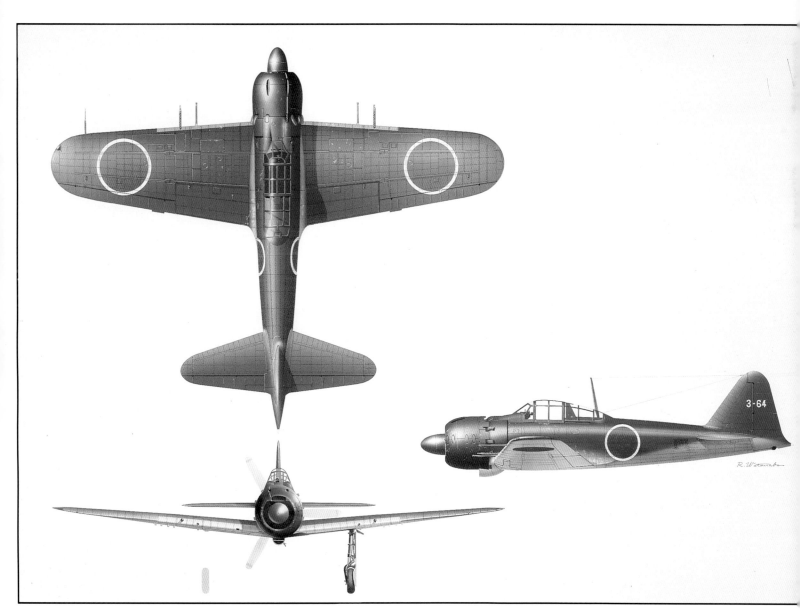

emergency replacement for the troublesome Aichi-built Atsuta inline water-cooled engine used on the carrier dive-bomber D4Y Judy, which was urgently needed in combat. Besides, the Navy claimed that the engineering time required for adapting this engine to the Zero airframe was prohibitive. As an alternate measure, the Navy recommended that water-methanol injection be used with the Sakae engine for emergency power. But the water-injected engine, now called the Sakae 31a, was slow in coming and the project had to continue with the existing series of the Sakae 21.

Nevertheless, the planned airframe modifications continued. When the first A6M5c was completed in September 1944, the flight test results were disappointing, but were expected under the circumstances. The added weight without increase in power reduced performance considerably. Production was interrupted with this model when the new A6M6c showed promise, but with its failing, A6M5c production was resumed until 93 models from this series were completed by the end of 1944.

A6M6c

By November of 1944, the water-injected Sakae 31a was installed in a Zero airframe under the project designation A6M6c, which also included installation of self-sealing fuel tanks. This new version would be the Model 53c, but it was never formally accepted by the Navy because it was a failure.

The new engine failed to perform as expected. Not only was the engine *reduced* in power due to the modification, but the new water-methanol metering system failed repeatedly during engine functional tests. A solution to the problem did not seem forthcoming, so the project was dropped after one example aircraft was produced.

As far as intended mission, armament, and armor are concerned, the Model 53c was the same as the Model 52c, and its designation followed the prescribed pattern for airframe and engine changes. The *c (Hei)* was tacked on to show that the offensive armament was the same as the Model 52c: three 13mm machine guns, two 20mm cannons, and four 66lb rocket bombs.

A6M7

The requirements for war continued to move ahead at a rate faster than Japan's aircraft industry could match. Deprived of its larger aircraft carriers by the fall of 1944, the Japanese Navy had difficulties in equipping its smaller carrier-borne units with suitable dive-bombers. The Aichi D3A Val was far too slow and virtually defenseless against new Allied fighters. Its replacement, the Aichi D4Y3 Judy, landed too fast to be safely operated from these carriers. A substitute had to be found in time to defend the Philippines against the coming Allied invasion.

The Model 52c aircraft then being turned out were modified for the fighter-bomber mission, while in the assembly plant under the project designation A6M7, Model 63. The armament remained the same as on the Model 52c, but the centerline drop tank was replaced by a Mitsubishi-designed bomb rack capable of carrying a 550lb bomb. Replacing the centerline fuel tank were two wing-mounted 40gal drop tanks fitted outboard of the landing gear.

The Zero Model 63 (A6M7) was a dive bomber version of the Zero. The centerline drop tank was replaced by a Mitsubishi-designed bomb rack capable of carrying a 550lb bomb. Rikyu Watanabe

To compensate for added stresses encountered in the dive-bomber role, thicker skin was added to the tail of these models.

Some measure of success must have been attained with the Sakae 31 series of engines since records do not show that this later airframe reverted to Sakae 21 engines. If this had happened, these would have been Zero Model 62s, but they were Model 63s of which the 3 indicates the later engine. One of three known examples of a Zero Model 63, which is in the US National Air and Space Museum in Washington, is fitted with a Sakae 31b engine according to the data plate and configuration. Mitsubishi produced an undetermined number of these models, starting their manufacture in May 1945. Zeros within this group included Model 62 with the Sakae 21 engine, according to Allied intelligence reports.

A6M8c

Despite the resistance of the JNAF to place a more powerful engine in the Zero airframe, a number of problems finally became evident. The aircraft continued to gain structural

Zero Model 63, A6M7. Changes for this model were mostly in the bomb racks for its fighter-bomber role. A Sakae 31b engine with water-methanol injection was installed. San Diego Aerospace Museum

weight with each modification, but little or no added power was ever introduced to compensate. In addition, the clean lines of the fighter were being interrupted with bomb racks, drop tanks, and more guns—all of which detracted from performance.

Another adverse circumstance had to do with the quality of the products. As the war dragged on, the quality of both airframes and engines suffered immensely. More and more, the factories were forced to rely upon unskilled and drafted labor. The relentless B-29 bombing raids added to this problem.

The greatest problem of all was the limited number of Sakae engines. Nakajima stopped making the Sakae in order to concentrate on the new Homare engine that was being used in so many new Army and Navy aircraft, including the Zero's intended replacement, the A7M Reppu (Sam). That left only the Ishikawajima company as a manufacturer of the Sakae. Consequently, the supply of Sakae engines became critically low.

As a result of all of these factors, the Navy agreed to try the Mitsubishi Kinsei 62 engine in the Zero. This combination had been Horikoshi's preference from the start, a Mitsubishi-built engine in a Mitsubishi airframe. The company was authorized to install the Kinsei in two suitably modified airframes from the current production output of A6M5c and A6M7 aircraft. The projected designation of this new design was Type Zero Carrier-Based Fighter Model 54c *(Rei Shiki Kanjo Sentoki Go Yon Hei Gata)*. The project short title was A6M8c.

The first prototype Model 54c was expected to be completed by the end of March 1945,

but extensive air-raid damage to the Mitsubishi dispersal plants delayed it. Engineers Eitaro Sano, Kazuaki Izumi, and Shiro Kushibe worked feverishly to deliver the aircraft on time and finally saw the first machine out of the factory in late April.

The new engine, being larger than the Sakae, required that the Zero's nose be scaled up to accommodate it, and the single fuselage-mounted 13mm machine gun had to be deleted.

Because of low quality of construction, the new engine suffered from such things as low oil pressure, high oil temperature, and fluctuations in fuel pressure at various altitudes. But these faults could by corrected, and in general the new design met the expectations of Mitsubishi and the Japanese Navy.

The Navy accepted the first A6M8c prototype on May 25, 1945, and one month later took delivery of the second. Maximum speed was recorded as 308kt at 19,700ft, along with the ability to climb to that altitude in 6min 50sec. Although this maximum level speed was 48kt slower than the F4U-1D at that altitude, it did halt the trend toward deteriorating performance that had prevailed since the spring of 1944. Japanese test pilots who flew the Model 54c overwhelmingly agreed that this was, so far, the best Zero model.

Satisfied with the promising results, the Navy laid overly optimistic plans to mass produce a refined variation of the Kinsei-engined Zero, rather than continue with the 54c as it was. The service ordered 6,300 machines for 1946. But none of these aircraft were completed before war's end. The design would have been known as the A6M8 Model 64.

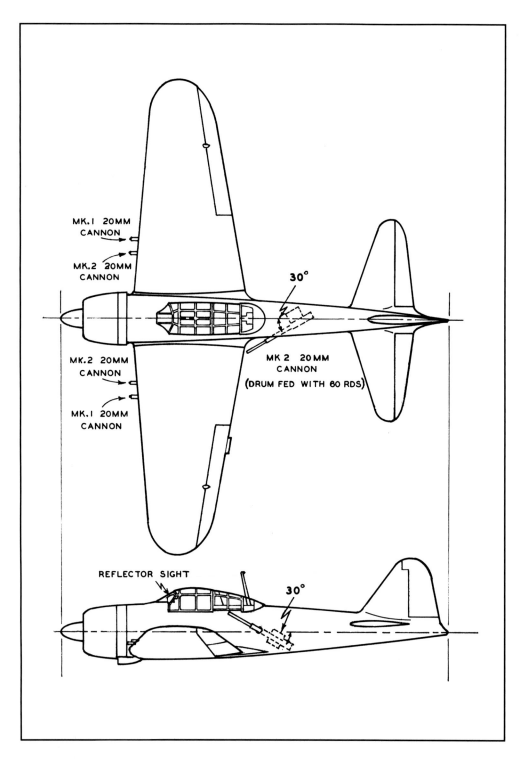

MK.1 20MM CANNON

MK.2 20MM CANNON

30°

MK 2 20MM CANNON (DRUM FED WITH 60 RDS)

MK.2 20MM CANNON

MK.1 20MM CANNON

REFLECTOR SIGHT

30°

Zero Night Fighter. This US intelligence drawing shows an oblique mounted cannon on an A6M5c Zero for night engagements, a method that proved quite practical. This variant did see operational use, notably with the 302nd Kokutai. It was also deployed overseas with 153rd Kokutai in the southern Philippines. Later models fired upward along the centerline.

Trainer Model, A6M2-K, and A6M5-K

Using the same airframe as the Model 21, modifications were made in the design to produce a tandem-seat transition trainer for Zero pilots. The A6M2-K design was accepted by the Navy for production as the Type Zero Training Fighter Model 11 (*Rei Shiki Renshu Sentoki Ichi Ichi Gata*).

Major components were sent from both Nakajima and Mitsubishi to the 21st Naval Air Depot (*Dai-Nijuinchi Kaigun Kokusho*) at Omura Air Station, Kyushu, and to Hitachi Aircraft Company at Haneda, Tokyo. At these locations, parts assembly took place producing not only these trainer versions, but fighter versions as well.

Noticeable features of the A6M2-K were the fixed open front cockpit and sliding hood arrangement for the rear cockpit. Wheel-well covers were eliminated, as were the 20mm wing cannon. Small horizontal fins were added to the rear of the fuselage to improve stability.

A more advanced version was developed at the 21st Naval Air Depot in August 1944. This became the A6M5-K, a two-seat version of the Model 52 Zero. The external difference to that of the A6M2-K was the Sakae 21 engine with short stacks and the shorter wing. Production of this version was passed to Hitachi Aircraft Company, their first being completed in March 1945. Records show that only seven of this model, plus prototypes, were built.

These trainer versions of the Zero served Navy fighter schools on the main islands of Japan with smaller quantities being sent overseas for pilot proficiency and target towing for gunnery.

A6M2-N

Coverage of the Zero would not be complete without mention of the floatplane version of the Zero called the Type 2 Seaplane Fighter (*Ni Shiki Suijo Sentoki*). While this designation does not indicate the Type Zero lineage, nevertheless it was basically the same Type Zero airframe with a flotation system attached.

Before the Pacific war began, Navy planners could see that a war was brewing and would involve all the forces of Japan. In planning for this eventuality that would cover the broad reaches of the Pacific, there would be a strong need for fighter support for the many planned island operations. In the absence of island airfields and aircraft carriers to support these operations, a seaplane fighter was thought to be the solution.

In September 1940, the Navy issued a specification to Kawanishi Aircraft Company for the 15-*Shi* High Speed Fighter Seaplane, an airplane that would be capable of swiftly reaching areas of operation where air support would be needed for Japanese amphibious landing forces. Kawanishi was the logical builder because of the promise that was foreseen in their development of the E15K Shiun high-speed reconnaissance float seaplane that was started a few months before.

Since this was to be an all-new design, the risk was too great to not have an interim seaplane fighter in a shorter period of time to fill this imminent need. The Navy BuAir decided to take an existing and proven fighter, namely the Zero, and create a floatplane conversion for expediency. Since Mitsubishi was heavily

Trainer Model, A6M2-K. The Navy and Hitachi Aircraft Company built two-seat trainer versions of the Zero, based upon the Model 21. These A6M2-K aircraft were used for pilot transitional training and target towing. Shoichi Tanaka

committed in production and Nakajima was more experienced in seaplane designs, Nakajima was awarded the Navy specification for the 15-*Shi* Fighter Seaplane. By this time, the Nakajima Koizumi Plant was in the tooling process as co-producer with Mitsubishi of the Zero, and therefore was ideal for production of the seaplane fighter version. Looked upon as a conversion only, it was initially known as the Mk.1 Fighter Seaplane, AS-1.

Placed in charge of this conversion project was Nakajima's Shinobu Mitsutake who would serve as chief designer. He was assisted by Engineer Tajima, also from the Nakajima staff. Their preliminary approach to the problem was to take the standard A6M2 airframe and make the following alterations.

First, remove the main landing gear and fair over the wheel wells. The wing design would remain that of the Model 11, which did not have the folding wing tip.

Second, a single all-metal centerline float would be attached to the main wing spar at the fuselage, with one forward sloping heavy pylon strut to be braced with a drag strut going from the one strut attach point on the float to the rear wing spar. This fore and aft aligned V-strut arrangement was faired over into a single pylon configuration. To stabilize the float, a V-strut would connect the aft portion of the float to the rear wing spar at the fuselage, offsetting the use of a drop tank that was normally mounted at the float attachment point. Internal fuel tanks were installed within the float itself. Wing-tip floats would be attached with a single strut.

Third, additional directional stabilizing surface would be needed because of the main float. This called for the redesign of the vertical fin and an extension of the rudder to the bottom of the fuselage. A stabilizing fin was

added under the tail at the rear of the fuselage.

The most unique feature of this float system was the single, main strut arrangement that held the centerline and wing-tip floats to the main spar of the wing. This configuration of float attachments had never been used on aircraft of this type anywhere in the world, and it provided the least drag of any fixed-type float arrangement.

On December 8, 1941, the first prototype of this conversion began its test flying. Testing became so accelerated that nearly all of the test program was completed in early 1942. By July 1942, the airplane was approved as an operational aircraft and placed into production as the Type 2 Seaplane Fighter Model 11. Its short designation was A6M2-N, the *N* signifying the mission of seaplane fighter. Eventually, it was given the code name of Rufe by the Allied intelligence.

Production of the Rufe was made on parallel lines with the standard Zero, since many parts were the same. Within the structure of the basic Zero design was a metal called *Elec-*

Type 2 Seaplane Fighter, A6M2-N. Nakajima modified the Zero that they were producing for the Navy, into an interim seaplane version.

tron (an aluminum-magnesium alloy). This metal proved to be highly susceptible to corrosion, a very undesirable quality for saltwater operations. Modifications were made in the seaplane version to use more corrosion-resistant metals, and to strengthen the fuselage and engine mount to better withstand hard impacts associated with alighting on water.

The Rufe's performance was less than that of the Zeke, but it was still a very capable fighter. It remained quite maneuverable in spite of being handicapped by the bulky, but streamlined main float. On the plus side, the design was not encumbered by the weight of the landing gear and its retraction mechanism, which partially offset the added weight of the float. As a result, the Rufe's overall empty weight was only 531lb heavier than the Model 21, a 14.3 percent increase. Following are some comparisons between the land-based Zeke 21 and the seaplane Rufe.

Deliveries began in mid-1942 to several naval *Kokutais*. Designed as an offensive fighter, the Rufe's mission became that of air defense, primarily. Their air operations were initially apparent when many were destroyed at their shore base on Tulagi Island in the Solomons by Allied pre-strike missions prior to the invasion of nearby Guadalcanal. Later, while assigned to the Japanese Fifth Fleet,

Rufe was the Allied code name given to this Type 2 Seaplane Fighter. Its design was uniquely streamlined for its time period because of the absence of supporting wires and multi-struts. National Archives

96

Model	Empty Weight	Loaded Weight	Maximum Speed	
Range				
Zeke 21	3,704lb	5,313lb	287kt	1,678nm
Rufe	4,235lb	5,423lb	234kt	960nm

Rufes were based on Kiska and Attu Islands off the Aleutians, providing air defense coverage for those Japanese outposts. They were felt later by Allied bombers when attacking the heavily fortified Japanese naval facility at Paramushir in the central Kurils from their seaplane base on Shimushu. They also served as escorts for reconnaissance seaplanes when assigned to special missions. The Rufe's service life was short, however, since land-based and carrier-based fighters were used wherever possible. There was a long period when they were not used operationally, but served as seaplane fighter trainers for future N1K1 Kyofu pilots. In the final months of the war, the Rufe's mission became air defense patrol over major naval bases in central-western Japan such as Sasebo, Kure, and Maizuru, the last base receiving air cover from the *Otsu Kokutai*, operating from Lake Biwa, north of Kyoto.

When comparing Rufe with other seaplane fighters, the later and more powerful Kawanishi N1K1 Kyofu, code named Rex, was a more effective fighter for the ground support roll. Rex remained the most effective seaplane fighter used operationally. Comparing Rufe with the experimental float-equipped Spitfire and Wildcat, Rufe certainly would be the better performer for the same reasons that the Zero outperformed these same two fighters early in the war.

Production continued from December 1941 to July 1943. Quantities of the Rufe have

often been a point of argument because of the authoritative *US Strategic Bombing Survey* quantity listing. In their monthly breakdown chart for fiscal year 1943, production (which ended in July) totaled 73. Someone inadvertently entered this figure in the September column as a total, but was also used as a September production which doubled 1943 production. Thus, when subtracting that extreme production figure of 73 for a single month, the quantity becomes a more believable number of 254 Rufe fighters.

Compendium

While Mitsubishi is the famous name behind the Zero since the design originated with them, it was Nakajima that built the greatest number of these airplanes. Both were heavily engaged in production of the Model 21 when Mitsubishi developed the Model 32, followed closely by the Model 22. Mitsubishi was the only manufacturer of these particular models. When the Model 52 was developed and accepted as an operational type, Mitsubishi placed this model in production first, followed by Nakajima and respective subcontractor companies. The Model 21 production did not end abruptly in favor of the Model 52, but continued until the major components in production, or on hand, were used. Nakajima continued building this model while Mitsubishi produced the Models 32 and 22.

Kawanishi N1K1 Kyofu was the ultimate in operational seaplane fighter designs. The A6M2-N Rufe was an interim airplane awaiting production of these aircraft code named Rex. Kawasaki was privileged by having the 1,460 hp Kasei engine to power this seaplane, while Nakajima was compelled to retain the 940hp Sakae 12 engine of the standard Zero fighter. This Kyofu belongs to the Otsu Kokutai.

Japan failed to see another of the improved models of the Zero come from their production lines. Time had run out and the surrender of Japan ended production. According to Jiro Horikoshi and Masatake Okumiya, co-authors of the book *The Zero Fighter*, neither the Navy nor the aviation companies understood the manpower requirements of aeronautical design under the stress of war. Those men charged directly with the continued development of the Zero were forced to dilute their energies because of unrealistic assignments to other projects. As they struggled to bring about a new fighter to replace the Zero, they failed to achieve original goals set for improvements to be made to the Zero. Had the Navy and the aircraft companies properly anticipated wartime engineering needs, the latest model of the Zero, Model 64, could have appeared at the front as early as the spring of 1943. If this had been the case, it could have done much to hold back the Hellcats, Corsairs, and Lightnings that sorely trounced the earlier generation Zeros that existed in the later war years.

A6M2-Ns saw service in the Aleutians and the Kurils in the early part of the war. In the Marshall Islands, pilots and ground crews of the 802nd Kokutai on Jaluit Atoll attend morning muster on May 27, 1943, by their newly received seaplanes.

Chapter 11

A Critical Look

In preparing this brief history of the Zero, already more than 50 years after its inception, it has been interesting to gather a number of viewpoints from different people concerning this airplane. Perhaps some of these insights were not even relevant at the time the Zero was in its prime.

One interesting account of the Zero was that expressed by a noted aeronautical engineer, the late Shizuo Kikuhara, designer of the Kawanishi H8K flying-boat known as Emily. With regard to the Zero's design, Kikuhara's commented on the airplane as "being full of foolish holes like swiss cheese." He was referring, of course, to the extreme measures that Zero designer Jiro Horikoshi went to in order to achieve lightness in the structure. Horikoshi achieved the design weight limit that he was striving for, but some like Kikuhara believed that he went too far and sacrificed needed strength.

In a more recent interview with Saburo Sakai, famed Zero ace, Sakai expressed his thoughts concerning the *best* and the *worst* aspects of the airplane. Referring specifically to the Model 21, Sakai commented that the Zero's long-range ability was its greatest asset. This, he attributed to its power-to-weight ratio. The engine power was the right selection for the light airframe. Referring to his notes, he reconfirmed that he once flew a Model 21 for 12hr, 5min. He was on a return flight to Taiwan, on which he intentionally flew the aircraft to dry-tanks over the field at 6,000ft and made a fast, gliding letdown for landing (his recorded time does not include

the glide or landing).

The Zero's worst features, according to Sakai, were its radios, and its lack of armor for the pilot or protection for the fuel tanks. These points are covered well in his 1950s book entitled *Samurai* (see appendices for details).

The same questions concerning the Zero's positive and negative points were asked of Ichiro Naito, noted Japanese aviation historian, aeronautical engineer, and in later years, highly respected teacher of aeronautics. During the war, Naito was a technical engineer at the Navy's test center, Kugisho, located at Yokosuka, where his duties also included flight evaluation of several aircraft. He described the Zero's features, both positive and negative, in one word—flimsy. Only because of its light weight, which in some ways compromised the structural strength of the air-

craft, did the Zero have its long-range capability, which he professed as being the Zero's best quality. This capability often placed the Japanese fighters at a battle scene when it otherwise would have been impossible to do so. "No other fighter compared in this aspect," said Naito. According to Naito, the Zero's long-range capability was possible as a result of a large aspect ratio wing and a low drag-to-power ratio.

The Sakae 12 engine was a "rarity," in Naito's words. Extraordinarily high in reliability, designed and built at a time when Japan could afford painstaking care in design and workmanship. These qualities helped ensure a very long range as well as endurance, features not normally found in other engines at that time, including the Japanese engines that followed.

A flight of A6M2s start engines in preparation for a training flight from Ohita Air Base on the northeast coast of Kyushu. This was a training base for Zero replacement pilots. Note the elevation of the pilot's seat for ease in ground taxiing. Shoichi Tanaka

A unique feature that worked well for the aircraft was the elasticity built into the control system for the elevator. This prevented the pilot from over-stressing the structure while at high G loads in combat maneuvers. Normally this would *induce* elevator flutter, but as sound engineering practices or pure luck would have it, the flutter did not happen in the case of the Zero!

Negative aspects aside, all of the aforementioned sources had deep admiration for this airplane as the ultimate solution for satis-fying the extreme requirements that were placed before designer Horikoshi.

Osamu Tagaya, a respected colleague, a true historian, and a highly regarded authority of Japanese aviation of World War II, expressed a different perspective about this airplane. Being one generation younger than those historians already mentioned, who formed their opinions about the Zero during wartime, Tagaya stated the following observations about Japanese armament, and how it affected the Zero.

Diverse Armament Concepts

The mid to late 1930s was a time when the world's air forces were making a major transition in the armament carried by their fighters. The difference in armament between the Zero and the US Navy's F4F Wildcat very much reflects the divergent philosophies of the two rival Pacific naval air forces.

The time period in question saw progressive development behind the classic pair of 7.7mm weapons which had been the standard on single-engine fighters since World War I.

The Planes of Fame A6M5 Zero. Planes of Fame

What emerged for nearly all US fighters of the 1940s was a battery of six or eight .50cal machine guns that became the hallmark of American fighters of World War II. (The British also adopted a pattern of multiple gun batteries of uniform bore in the late 1930s, but standardized on .303cal weapons.)

This makes an interesting contrast with the pattern adopted in the Axis countries. The JNAF made a leap in gun bore from 7.7mm to 20mm, skipping the 13mm (i.e., .50cal) size altogether. This was identical to the pattern adopted by the German Luftwaffe in the Bf 109E-3. It was not until much later that the JNAF came to recognize the merits of the 13mm weapon and developed it.

(The JAAF went from 7.7mm to 13mm first, before adopting 20mm cannons. They maintained a mixed caliber armament pattern in their fighters and did not subscribe to the American pattern of multi-gun batteries of uniform caliber.)

What is important to keep in mind with respect to the Zero is that the 20mm cannon installed in the A6M2 did not produce the results expected. Certainly if an explosive shell from one of these guns hit its target, the effect was devastating. Therefore, it was undoubtedly a powerful weapon—technically. But in practice the low muzzle velocity and short effective trajectory of the gun, coupled initially with its very meager magazine capacity of 60 rounds, significantly limited its effectiveness until improved later.

In a conversation that Tagaya had with Saburo Sakai on the subject of armament, Sakai exclaimed that although the Type 99 Mk.1 cannon was effective when it could be used correctly, most of the aerial victories achieved by A6M2 Zero pilots during the crucial first six months of the war were being attained with the cowl-mounted 7.7mm types. Sakai made it clear that, in his opinion, the American policy of multiple .50cal guns was the correct one.

The American pattern was ideal, according to Tagaya. The .50cal gun afforded much greater destructive power than .30cal weapons, while at the same time having faster rates of fire and much longer effective trajectory than a 20mm cannon, given the technology of the time.

Zero Fighter designer Jiro Horikoshi achieved the airframe weight limitations within structural strength parameters, but when subjected to the rigors of severe combat against Allied aircraft, his creation would not withstand the punishment. The survivor shown here was recovered from Ballale in the Solomon Islands in the 1960s, and after rebuilding, now flies with the Confederate Air Force. The markings on this A6M2 are representative of the aircraft on the carrier Zuikaku *at the time of the Pearl Harbor Attack. Brian M. Silcox*

The Zero was one of the first fighters in the world to incorporate a centerline fuel tank as part of its initial design. The fuel in this tank was used first, then the tank was dropped and actually fired away by strong springs so that the tank would not be an aerodynamic drag or a fire hazard during combat. Two standard sizes were 320ltr and 330ltr (about 84 and 87gal).

It has been stressed, and quite correctly, that the practice of US Navy aerial gunnery in World War II was deflection shooting. More than any other air service, the US Navy drilled its fighter pilots in this art as standard procedure. In contrast, the Japanese have often been accused of being simple-minded tail chasers who relied on the phenomenal maneuverability of their mounts to get them in a good firing position. Like all myths, this has both a grain of truth and elements of fiction.

Deflection shooting was by no means unknown to JNAF fighter pilots. The more skilled and experienced among them were adept at it, and practiced it regularly like their US Navy counterparts. What is not often pointed out, however, is that certain armament patterns are much more conducive than others when putting deflection shooting into practice. Obviously, it is easier to do so with a concentrated battery of guns with uniform trajectory and firing pattern, than it is with mixed-caliber armament in which the guns

have different trajectory envelopes and rates of fire. This, in itself, creates two target tracking problems for one air engagement, as opposed to using only one size weapon in a battery format.

In modern warfare, *quantity* of production is often as important as and sometimes more important than *quality* of production. This goes for men as well as machines. Uniform-caliber armament ensured a higher proportion of good gunnery among pilots of average quality than did mixed-caliber armament. In adopting 20mm armament for the Zero, the JNAF focused on increasing destructive power in the narrow technical sense. In contrast, the US air forces achieved greater destructive power in terms of practical application by adopting uniform-caliber armament. The Japanese system was formidable so long as highly skilled pilots were available. As the war progressed, however, and both sides had to rely on mass-conscripted pilot trainees, it was the American system that prevailed. At

Grumman F4F-3 Wildcats were designed without pilot protection or bulletproof fuel tanks. When this need became apparent, the United States was able to make these modifications to existing aircraft more quickly than was Japan.

By the end of the war, the Zero was outfitted with the ultimate armament package for the design. The two 20mm wing cannons had been augmented with two 13mm machine guns beginning with the A6M5c. The two 7.7mm guns formerly in the fuselage were replaced by one 13mm in the right hand position. Wing racks for small air-to-air rocket bombs and a centerline rack for a large bomb were added. Shoichi Tanaka

that point, the average quality of American pilots surpassed that of the Japanese. This, coupled with the unquestioned numerical superiority of US troops, meant that the handwriting was on the wall for the Japanese.

Another fact concerning the A6M2 and its 20mm cannon illustrates the tenuous production capabilities with which the Japanese challenged the American industrial giant of the 1940s. Production of the Oerlikon-licensed Type 99 20mm Mk. 1 was entrusted to *Dai Nihon Heiki KK*. Production, however, was exceedingly slow due to limited capacity, so much so that when Admiral Chuichi Nagumo's carriers sailed for Hawaii, they did so with only two or three spare 20mm guns for all of the Zeros on board each flat-top.

Self-Sealing Tanks and Armor

When questioned about protective qualities built into the Zero and other Japanese aircraft, Osamu Tagaya expressed some new concepts that few Westerners understood during wartime. The lack of self-sealing fuel tanks and pilot armor are usually cited as the main weaknesses of Japanese warplane design dur-

ing World War II. However, this statement can be broadly misconstrued.

It is true that the Japanese were among the last major combatants in World War II to adopt these features on their aircraft, and the lack of them put Japanese warplanes at a distinct disadvantage in air combat. But this reflects operational philosophy on the part of Japan's air services rather than any inherent defect in aircraft design. The issue goes beyond just the Zero, of course, and applies to all major Japanese warplanes conceived and designed in the late 1930s. Reading the standard literature on the subject, one gains the impression that the Japanese stand out like a "sore thumb" in not providing these features while everyone else did. This simply is not true. It should be pointed out that the Zero's contemporaries around the world, and just about all other combat aircraft of that period, originally were conceived as machines that would be flown in combat without armor or self-sealing fuel tanks and were designed accordingly. The truth of the matter is that in the mid-1930s, neither aircraft designers nor, more importantly, air force officers who were responsible for

A Zero, as seen during an attack by an American fighter, through the lens of the gun camera. National Archives

formulating design specifications to be imposed on aircraft manufacturers and their design staffs, foresaw the importance of these features in a future war. Changes in attitude came, not as a result of someone's farsightedness, but through harsh combat experience. In Europe, where war came first (China should be discounted, given the generally weak nature of the opposition), the Hurricane, Spitfire, and Bf 109E all began combat without armor or self-sealing fuel tanks. It was not until the

tough, evenly matched combat experienced by the two sides during the Battle of Britain that these features became widely adopted. Some Luftwaffe units had armor installed in their aircraft in June-July 1940, before the Battle of Britain, as may have some RAF units. Regardless of who should be credited for being the "first," these features did not become standard in front-line aircraft until the latter part of 1940.

In the United States—after witnessing Great Britain's experience in the Battle of Britain, as well as the ongoing developments in the European air war—opinion began to favor self-sealing fuel tanks and armor protection for the pilot during 1940 and into 1941. At

this time, the US Navy fighter squadrons on the East Coast had just begun to receive self-sealing tanks for their F4F-3s. As with anything, however, implementation took time, and many US aircraft, including F4F-3s in the Pacific, did not have these features at the time of Pearl Harbor.

In light of these comparisons, the unprotected nature of the Zero and other Japanese aircraft of the period does not seem particularly out of place. The fault, if there is any, certainly does not lie with the aircraft designers. Where a major difference does exist is in the way the two opponents' approached the situation. By December 1941, the US air services had already clearly identified the need for

these protective features, and were in the process of providing them, albeit incompletely at the time the Japanese struck. Therefore, once the war in the Pacific began, the vast majority of American aircraft had these features within a relatively short period of time. As for the Japanese, they were by no means oblivious to the issue of aircraft protection. Already, during the China war, combat units pointed out the need for and the efficiency of providing fuel tank protection, and some preliminary studies were made in developing such tanks.

It was not until after the Pacific war began, specifically not until the Guadalcanal Campaign got under way, when American opposition stiffened and attrition among Japanese air units mounted alarmingly, that the urgency was felt. Had they begun as early as 1940, Japan could have learned through the experience of others who fought the war in Europe. Instead, they gave credence to their own direct combat experience in China, from which they drew the wrong conclusions and gained an arrogant self-confidence. Also, the totalitarian nature of the German and Japanese governments probably hampered a free and open exchange of information. By waiting until forced to react to the harsh realities of combat, the Japanese were no different than the other combatant nations.

Once the need was identified, however, it took the Japanese almost a year to develop and install effective self-sealing fuel tanks in their aircraft. Pilot armor and bulletproof glass came even later. It was not until late 1943 that

Many battles were lost by the Zero for its lack of ability to sustain battle damage so that it could fight another day. The added weight for armor and self-sealing fuel tanks was sacrificed on Japanese aircraft in the early part of the war in favor of performance. National Archives

A retrofit to the design of the Zero were these balancing tabs added to the inboard ends of both ailerons. These were to relieve control forces experienced by pilots at high maneuvering speeds. With this came a wing flutter at a lower airspeed than before which brought about an airspeed restriction. As designer Horikoshi later pointed out, part of the problem was that these tabs were not blended into the overall design of the original aircraft.

Japanese aircraft attained the level of protection enjoyed by US aircraft as early as mid-1942. By then, of course, what thin margin of advantage the Japanese may have enjoyed initially had been irretrievably lost. This failure on the part of the Japanese to quickly develop effective self-sealing tanks can be attributed to the nation's limited technological capabilities in the 1940s.

As aptly stated by Tagaya in describing the situation in today's terms, to a younger postwar audience that finds itself surrounded by Sony TV sets and Toyota cars, this may sound surprising. One must be reminded that the Japan of the 1930s and 1940s was trying desperately to impose a military industrial complex from a high level of government on what essentially was still an agrarian and light industrial society that had just emerged from feudalism less than a century before. In their bid to become a major power, the Japanese of that period achieved some great successes and produced some sophisticated weaponry, but there were big gaps in technology in various fields. This stemmed from the fact that industrialization essentially had been imposed from the top down, directed and financed to a large extent by the central government, rather than growing from the bottom up in the society, as it had in the US and Western Europe. Therefore, according to Tagaya, while certain targeted sections of industry could produce internationally competitive products, the general standard of living and economic infrastructure significantly lagged behind the West. In short, the Japan of that time was similar to the Soviet Union or many of the Third World countries today.

This weakness of the industrial infrastructure manifested itself in many ways. One was the inability of Japanese industry to produce a high-grade rubber material of consistent quality and in industrial quantities. This was the key reason for the delay in developing self-sealing tanks in Japan.

Another factor, and one that explains why the Japanese took longer than other nations in confronting the aircraft protection problem, was psychological. Although irrational from the modern perspective, Tagaya explains, the traditional Samurai psyche still permeated much of Japanese society in those days, especially within the two services. Part of that tradition maintained that a warrior should always be ready to accept death in an honorable fashion. Therefore anything that smacked of trying to save one's skin, such as armor plate, was frowned upon. Another prevalent attitude was that of always demanding the utmost performance from one's aircraft. Combat pilots, far from demanding better protection for their aircraft, more often complained that addition of armor and fuel tank self-sealing material would adversely affect aircraft performance. It was not uncommon for pilots to leave their parachutes on the ground in order to reduce weight for an added advantage in an air duel. Given their underlying attitudes toward death in combat, they tended to see such protective features as an unnecessary luxury rather than essential protection. It took wholesale attrition to make them realize that in modern warfare, surviving to fight again another day was ultimately in the better interest of one's nation other than *going out in a blaze of glory!*

The point must be stressed, however, that the lack of pilot and armor protection was not an oversight by the designers. What was missing from the very beginning was a good 1,200hp engine to carry the necessary safeguards for aircraft and pilot without sacrificing performance. As was the case with Allied planes, more power should have been added

This diagram of the balancing tab was traced from Technical Air Intelligence Summary No.7, January 1944, in which the operation of the tab was described. The graphic shows how the tabs are rendered inoperative by aligning the connecting arm point C with the aileron hinge axis F when the flaps are down . Conversely when the flaps are retracted, the bell crank arm is repositioned, displacing C as shown, causing the tabs to deflect when the aileron is moved. O.P..35-7 14, Dec.1943.

A temporary retrofit that delayed aileron flutter until a higher speed was the addition of this counterbalance weight at the end of the aileron up through airframe No. 326. Shoichi Tanaka

over the years as the Zero was improved with its inherent weight penalties. Horikoshi did extremely well with the limited horsepower that was available to him for the Zero.

About Those Tabs . . .

Much has been written about *tabs* on the Zero because the subject played so prominently in the early development of the Zero, associated with the second fatal accident. From this has stemmed frequent, and sometimes erroneous references about tabs, enough so that some explanation is required here to clarify some points.

In reference to the balancing tabs introduced on the Model 21, on the 127th and later aircraft, these were located inboard on the trailing edges of both ailerons. They were mechanically linked so that when the aileron was moved by stick force, the tabs moved in the

opposite direction and provided an air load that assisted in this movement of the aileron. This increased the Zero's maneuverability which, on earlier models, was particularly sluggish at high speeds.

While this control assist was good, designers felt that there would be a tendency to overcontrol in the lateral plane of movement at the slower speed range, such as in the landing pattern. To preclude this from happening, Zero designer Jiro Horikoshi incorporated into this linkage a system whereby the tabs became inoperative in the more critical landing pattern speed range. In two places in his book *The Zero Fighter*, he explains that this was possible when they "installed on the ailerons new balancing tabs which were linked with the gear-retracting mechanism . . ." and further described as ". . . attach balancing tabs to the ailerons, which became inoperative when the landing gear was lowered, therefore preserving the original 'feel' at low speeds."

The theory and concept described here is certainly valid. However, there is a technical variance. Drawings of the A6M2 wing flap make note that from the 127th aircraft, this ac-

tivation mechanism was attached to a fitting on the outboard end of the flap, not the landing gear.

The short-wing version of the Zero that followed, Model 32, somewhat eliminated the need for this balancing tab arrangement. Being a shorter wing, the role rate was naturally faster, and having a smaller aileron as well, the stick pressure was not as great.

But the problem returned when the Zero design reverted back to the original longer span wing with the introduction of the Model 22. Technical Air Intelligence Summary No. 7, dated January 1944, describes in detail the operation of this tab movement after inspecting Model 22s when the Allies occupied Cape Gloucester on New Britain. Their description and graphic showed that linkage from the landing flap (when extended 30 degrees or more) mechanically neutralized the operation of the tabs regardless of aileron deflection, thus eliminating overcontrol.

With regard to landing gear linkages, several publications have confused this balance trim system with that of a flap or door operation below the wing cannon. The linkage, described particularly for the A6M5c, opens a cover for the cartridge-link ejection tube when the gear is retracted, and closes the cover

Rudder trim tabs did not appear on Zeros until sometime in mid-production of the Mitsubishi-built A6M3 Model 22. They were standard on all subsequent aircraft.

Cockpit of the restored A6M5 in the National Air and Space Museum. Instrument positions sometimes varied by the choice of the pilot. The pilot charged the two machine guns, seen in each upper corner, by pulling the cocking levers toward him, just as was done on World War I fighters.

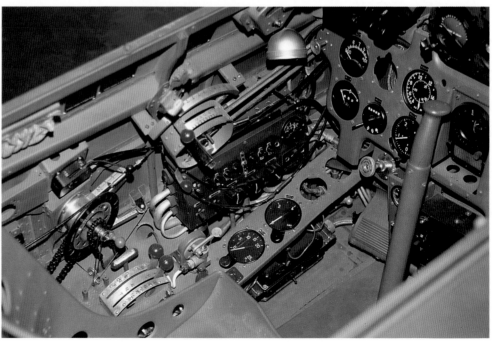

Throttle quadrant and fuel gauges are seen in the left of the cockpit. Rudder trim wheel is positioned beside and to the left of the seat.

when the gear is down. This prevents dirt and debris from clogging the chute when operating from the normally unprepared airfields.

Returning once again to tabs, the operation of trim tabs has varied from ground adjustable only, to pilot adjustable from inside the cockpit. Aileron trims, when installed, were always those of balancing tabs, with a hand-bendable tab used for ground adjustable trim. This was true with rudder trim as well, until the Model 22, for which at some point in its production period a cockpit-adjustable trim tab was introduced and appeared on all models that followed. All models had a cockpit-adjustable elevator trim tab for pitch control, located inboard on each of the two control surfaces.

An oddity with the Zero was that when lowering the landing flaps, the nose pitched up, requiring nose-down trim, an opposite reaction from that of most other aircraft. Planned or unplanned, this accounts for the relatively small size elevator in the Zero design. If the usual pitch-down occurred with the Zero when extending the flaps, a much larger elevator would have been necessary for adequate control to achieve a three-point landing attitude. A larger elevator then would have further aggravated the overcontrol problem at high speed, which Horikoshi resolved with stretch control cables. So many design factors hinge on one another that it makes one far more appreciative of the design genius that made the Zero successful.

From the Cockpit

There are a number of interesting details that arise only when making a thorough comparison of the various Zero models, many of which are hardly noted elsewhere. For instance, early models had a full-swivel tail wheel, but beginning with the Model 32, a tail wheel lock was installed. From the cockpit, the pilot moved a lever at his lower left that allowed a spring-loaded pin to drop into the front end of the steering horn, which holds the tail wheel straight during takeoff and landing. This probably became necessary because of the added engine torque of the Sakae 21 engine. According to Dr. John Kelley, sponsor of the Confederate Air Museum (CAF)'s A6M2, the tail wheel is steerable by cables from the rudder through an arc of about 60 degrees, but full swiveling can be accomplished by giving the tail a sharp sideways *kick* with brake pressure to one wheel, which overrides the dogs tending to keep it within the normal arc.

Cockpit layouts are obviously of keen interest to pilots. In the case of the Zero, it was not unlike a lot of aircraft in having the landing gear and flap controls on the *wrong* side of the cockpit, meaning on the right. The left hand is normally kept on the throttle control on the left side of the cockpit. This caused the pilot to take his hand off the throttle, change hands holding the stick, position the gear and

The Zero's cockpit was snug by Western standards, yet was quite functional. Few details differed from Allied fighters, making the transition to flying this former enemy aircraft for evaluation quite routine.

The red pad on the reflector gunsight protects the pilot during crash landings. To the right, out of sight in this view, are the landing gear and flap handles.

Those who study the evolution of aircraft designs invariably come to believe that the Zero had some special ingredient. Whatever that was—be it design balance, style, or engineering genius—because of it, this airplane will stand apart from all others. Planes of Fame

flap handles with the right hand, and then transfer back again. This is awkward during the critical takeoff and landing phase of the flight, but one gets used to it. Hydraulic lines connecting these controls made them too bulky to fit on the left side of the cockpit with the engine controls and related linkages.

American pilots flying the Zero found the mixture controls on the power quadrant unorthodox. The throttle and propeller control handles operated in the direction they were used to, but the mixture control handles, of which there were two, moved in the opposite direction. From the full aft position for full rich at takeoff, the control was moved forward to a position opposite a number on the quadrant, equal to the altitude in thousands of feet. Adjacent to this control handle was the manual mixture control. Once the automatic mixture handle reached its full range, this control was moved forward to further lean the mixture.

In general terms, there was little else that was noticeably different about the cockpit arrangement and the flying of the Zero. Most American pilots would make the comment that it was a fairly snug cockpit, but not so for Japanese stature at that time. With heavy flight clothing on an American pilot, the cockpit was fairly crowded, which made reaching for and seeing the controls and instruments at the lower sides of the cockpit difficult. Otherwise, pilots had much more praise for than criticism about the flying and handling qualities of the Zero.

John Kelley, one of the sponsors and pilots of the CAF Zero, had this to say about flying the Japanese fighter plane:

"Because of the cramped cockpit for the bigger guys, control stick movement was actually limited at times. The rudder is so small that takeoff with a cross wind is 'very interesting'; often full right rudder is not enough and a tap on the brake is needed to keep it lined down the runway. Carrier approach landings are best if you like seeing the runway! Approach speeds are under 90kt, forward visibility is blocked by the higher angle of the nose. So you make a choice of priorities. At 90kt over the numbers, it needs 4,000ft of runway with flaps down; at 80kt, you can turn off inside 3,000ft. In general, the Zero is a sweet little airplane to fly, having no noticeable bad habits."

Was the Zero a Copy?

Even today, there are those who will argue that the Zero was a copy of aircraft like the Hughes Racer, or the Vought 143, and that it incorporated design concepts of other aircraft. The Zero was, as we now know, a completely original design. No one more vigorously defended that position than the designer himself, Jiro Horikoshi. That would be a natural position to take, but the points he makes are well supported. In words expressed long before his death on January 11, 1982

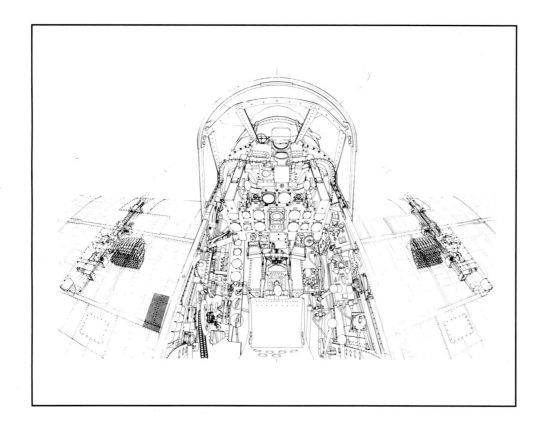

Zero cockpit details. Rikyu Watanabe

Features that identify this as a Model 52 from this angle include a tapered and pointed aileron to the wing tip, and the rear-set oil cooler back from the forward part of the engine cowling. The slightly protruding fairings just inboard of the two (only) wing guns cover the ammunition drums. These drums and fairings were eliminated on the A6M5a, which had belt-fed cannon. USAF

(Horikoshi died of pneumonia in a Tokyo hospital at age 78), this was his response to a very old controversy:

"The Zero Fighter was no more a copy than any other fighter used in the world today. All single-engine all-metal low-wing monoplanes are to some extent progressive 'copies' of the original Junkers 'Blechesel,' the father of all these machines. There is a certain pool of common information from which all engineers draw. There is a certain reciprocal borrowing of detail ideas without permission during wartime, and by cross-licensing in times of peace.

"As virtually all competent aircraft designers will hold with me, the business of creating any new airplane is a process of adapting the existing art and science to the problem at hand. For example, I will state that the undercarriage retraction on the Zero was inspired by the Vought 143, and that the system of fastening the engine cowl and the method of mounting the engine came from other foreign planes. And nothing else, so far as the airframe is concerned. It is no exaggeration to say that we did not look upon the general design or basic configuration of foreign aircraft with great respect. Any designer who fails, out of vanity, to adapt the best techniques available to him, fails his job. All engineers are influenced by their teachers, by their experience, and by the constant stream of scientific information that is placed at their disposal."

Horikoshi continued: "As foreigners inspected our aircraft in the combat zone, they were quick to identify accessories that looked familiar to them as copies of their own products. What they did overlook was that these

were built under license from abroad; wheels were manufactured by Okamoto Engineering Company under license from Bendix and Palmer, instruments were built by the Tokyo Instrument Company under license, or later in the war, by direct copy from Sperry, Pioneer, and Kollsman. Sumitomo built hydromatic propellers under a license from Hamilton Standard, as well as the German VDM propeller. The Nihon Musical Instrument Company built the Junkers and Schwarz propellers, while the Kokusai Aircraft Company built the French Ratier prop. We built 20mm cannon licensed by Oerlikon of Switzerland and copies of the 13mm (.50cal) Browning.

"I can claim, however, in the study of the Zero, its ancestors and descendants, that it was original in the same degree as other planes are, and that while it contains certain special features that were all its own, it serves as a prime example of a special design created to suit an unusual set of circumstances."

Chapter 12

Zero Fighter Serial Numbers

by James I. Long

It was natural for Allied intelligence organizations during World War II to seek an understanding of Japanese aircraft serial numbers as part of their task in assessing Japan's industrial potential to build aircraft. Frequent encounters with wreckage of Zeros focused attention on these aircraft for uncovering intelligence information. Ironically, it has only been in recent years that a full understanding of their serial numbering system has been unsnarled, discovering not one encoding system, but several for the various models and manufacturers of Zeros. For the first time in published form, these mysteries are explained.

This typical Japanese naval aircraft nameplate came from the cockpit wall of the Zero acquired in the Aleutians, and tested by Americans at San Diego. It reads as follows:
Place of Manufacture: Mitsubishi Heavy Industry Company, Nagoya Aircraft Factory.
Name: Type Zero Mark 1 Carrier-based Fighter Model 2.
Model-type: A6M2.
Engine: Nakajima NK1 ( ) hp.
Production [serial] Number: No. 4593.
Net Weight: 1715.0 Kilograms.
Load: 650.3 Kilograms.
Full Flight Weight: 2365.3 Kilograms.
Completion Date: February 19, 1942.
Inspection Mark: (Na Ko) (Naval Anchor).

Before the attack on Pearl Harbor on December 7, 1941, little or no thought was given to this type of information by the sparse intelligence community. After the attack, the remains of crashed enemy aircraft were examined for any information that might reveal part numbers, s/ns, equipment type and model—anything that would lead to production frequency and locations.

When intelligence specialists were first confronted with the task of analyzing specific s/ns, they were baffled. Their tabulations of s/ns and corresponding production dates made no sense at all. Some aircraft had numerically low s/ns with recent dates of assembly, while other aircraft of the same type and with the same operational history had numerically higher s/ns and much earlier assembly dates.

The reason for this apparent random allotment of s/ns was rooted in the Japanese military's penchant for tight security. The JAAF and JNAF were well aware that systematic and overt aircraft serializing would give a potential enemy the key to valuable intelligence information on production rates, quantities, factory locations, distribution times, modifications, technical difficulties, and other details related to aircraft production and deployment. To hinder an enemy's efforts to obtain such information, the Japanese military services and the Japanese aircraft industry collaborated to conceal the simple s/ns by applying a variety of encoding measures that added meaningless digits, but nevertheless ensured that their own personnel would recognize and be able to use the numbers.

The intelligence-gathering effort that began after the Pearl Harbor attack and the recovery of a crashed Zero (s/n 5289 built August 9, 1941) was stalemated until February 24, 1942, when another crashed Zero was recovered on Melville Island near Port Darwin. Though it was demolished, and thus not a candidate for flight testing, it nevertheless gave up some of its secrets. Intelligence personnel discovered that the plane's s/n was Mitsubishi No. 5349, that its model-type designation was Type 0 Carrier-Fighter Mk. 1-2 (A6M2), and that it was completed on October 4, 1941.

At that early date, the technical intelligence officers could not place any significance upon the s/n 5349. But obviously, everyone hoped that it was not a straightforward series production number, which would mean that the Japanese had built at least 5,349 Zeros! Equally perplexing was the knowledge that the s/n (1575) from a crashed Zero on New Guinea was nearly 4,000 less than the s/n (5289) of the crashed Zero examined at Pearl Harbor that was built six months earlier.

Crash inspectors who examined the wrecks became aware that Nakajima was also assembling the Zero. So in addition to the Mitsubishi numbers already mentioned, there were a few s/ns from Nakajima-built A6M2 Zeros, with characteristics altogether different from those of the Mitsubishi aircraft, such as 911, 916, 645, and 8328.

Supplementing the cockpit nameplate in identification was this stencil that was applied to the aft fuselage of Japanese naval aircraft. This marking on the side of the same Zero acquired from the Aleutians was painted just forward of the left horizontal stabilizer. Its data is as follows:
Model-type: Type Zero Mark 4 Carrier-based Fighter Model 2.
Production [Serial] Number: Mitsubishi No. 4593.
Production Date: February 19, 1942.
Assigned [to]: (left blank)
USAF Museum

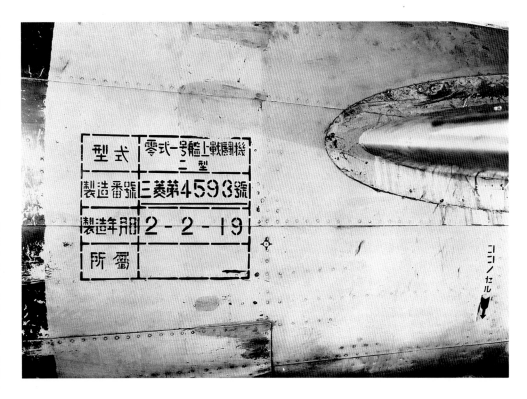

Mitsubishi Serial Numbers Deciphered

A break in the interpretation of s/ns came in late December 1942. This occurred when advancing Allied soldiers ran across 12 examples of a fighter with square-tipped wings when they captured the airstrip near Buna Mission on New Guinea. These were A6M3s, a new model of the Zero. Although they were Zeros, their s/ns appeared to have an altogether different format from that of the earlier A6M2 Zeros.

The revelation was that all were consistent four-digit numbers beginning with 3, and that the numbers that followed were closely related as well as sequenced in line with construction dates. The analysts reasoned, therefore, that the 3 was an identifier for the A6M3, and that as a cipher, it could be dropped to reveal the true s/n. Only Mitsubishi constructed A6M3 Zeros; therefore, a Nakajima serial counterpart problem was not encountered.

This breakthrough gave encouragement that the entire Japanese encoding system could be broken. To solve the remaining mysteries for other serial-number coding, analysts pooled all of the Mitsubishi A6M2 s/ns for comparison. In so doing, they noted a peculiar consistency. Whenever the last digit of any of these numbers was a 0 or 6, the first digit was a 1. Whenever the last digit was a 1 or 7, the first digit was a 2. If the last digit was a 2 or 8, the first digit was a 3, and so forth. The pattern became as systematic as was the one for the A6M3.

This discovery led analysts to conclude that, as with the previous decoding of A6M3 airplane numbers, the first digit of Mitsubishi A6M2 numbers could be ignored to find the true s/n. It was a theory that easily answered the old question of why A6M2 No. 5289 found at Pearl Harbor had an earlier assembly date than did A6M2 No. 1575 found in New Guinea.

Analysts felt that what was being used at the Mitsubishi factory to assign s/ns was something like a four-wheel numbering machine—something similar to an automobile odometer. On it, the units, tens, and hundreds wheels worked normally.

But the thousands wheel progressed each time the *units* wheel turned, and the former had only the digits 1 through 5, repeated once to make ten digits. In practice, the numbering looked like the following, inserting the tens and hundreds digits (shown below as X) as necessary to consecutively assign s/ns.

1XX0	1XX5
2XX1	2XX6
3XX2	3XX7
4XX3	4XX8
5XX4	5XX9

The intelligence team named this method of numbering the Mitsubishi 5-Cycle Code System. They reported that it applied to four-digit A6M2 s/ns, whether from an airframe or component.

This code structure was good for true s/n 100 and above. For s/ns less than 99, Mitsubishi had yet another system for these one- and two-digit s/ns, called an eight-cycle code system (see chart). This was more complicated than the five-cycle variety previously discussed. The system made three-digit coded s/ns by adding a code digit to the hundreds position, selected from a repeating sequence of the numerals 2 through 9. The eight-cycle code system precludes simple rule statements of how prefix numbers were assigned, making a tabulation the best way to see the code assignment (see the sidebar for more information).

Mitsubishi Eight-Cycle Coding System

To establish s/ns for aircraft with c/ns 99 and below, Mitsubishi used the eight-cycle coded numbering system. (Two examples are in bold type in the table: aircraft with visible s/ns **358** and 605).

False Digit
Prefix True C/N

2	(0)1	(0)9	17	25	33	41	49	57	65	73	81	89	97
3	(0)2	10	18	26	34	42	50	**58**	66	74	82	90	98
4	(0)3	11	19	27	35	43	51	59	67	75	83	91	99
5	(0)4	12	20	28	36	44	52	60	68	76	84	92	
6	**(0)5**	13	21	29	37	45	53	61	69	77	85	93	
7	(0)6	14	22	30	38	46	54	62	70	78	86	94	
8	(0)7	15	23	31	39	47	55	63	71	79	87	95	
9	(0)8	16	24	32	40	48	56	64	72	80	88	96	

Source: Naval Air Headquarters (Mitsubishi Heavy Industries). Type Zero Mk. 1 Carrier Fighter Models 1 and 2 (Airplane No. 6 and above).

Mitsubishi A6M5 and A6M8 Serial Numbers

The JNAF and aircraft manufacturers had decided to let the coded s/ns progress in an unbroken sequence to the foreseeable end of production of the A6M series. By now, production had advanced into the A6M5 series and the 3 prefix discovered from the A6M3 series had extended into the next Zero model, advancing from the A6M3 to the A6M5. Consequently, A6M5 No. 3999 signaled the end of coded s/ns with 3s as the first digit. The next A6M to be completed bore coded s/n 4000, and brought down the curtain on three-digit true s/ns. Thus, from airplane No. 4000 to the final Mitsubishi-built Zero, one need only to subtract 3000 from a coded number in order to derive the true number. The true s/n of what appeared as No. 4000 was, therefore, not 000, but 1000; No. 4001 was actually 1001, and so on.

Nakajima A6M5 and A6M7 Serial Numbers

When Nakajima changed production from the A6M2 to the more advanced models beginning in February 1944, the company started over with their s/ns. Beginning with coded s/n 11 for the first A6M5, once again they used the ten-cycle system. Coded s/ns from the entire range of A6M5 through A6M7 production ran from No. 11 through No. 33573.

21st Naval Air Arsenal A6M2-K Serial Numbers

The 21st Naval Air Arsenal at Omura, Kyushu, built the two-seat A6M2-K, known as the Type Zero Training Fighter, from January 1943 through October 1944. The true s/ns were 1 through 238. Researchers have not found any examples of coded s/ns for these trainers, and do not know how—or even if—the true numbers were encoded.

Hitachi Aircraft Company A6M2-K Serial Numbers

Hitachi began production of the A6M2-K in May 1944 and produced 279 airplanes, a figure thought to include seven A6M5-K aircraft as well. Researchers have reported one coded s/n: 2263. This fragmentary evidence, if correct, indicates encoding by adding 2000 to each true s/n, or by adding a 2 to each true number, or by adding various digits from a cyclic code keyed, say, to the unit's digit. One example s/n, however, cannot reveal which method Hitachi used.

A later form of data block was photographed on an aircraft captured on Saipan in June 1944 by Allied forces. It has a rarely seen entry on the bottom line. Mitsubishi used the standard four-line stencil until 1943, which included an assembly-date line for the airframe, but dropped it when the Japanese Navy forbade displays of such dates in November 1942. The stencil displays the following information: Model-type: Type Zero Carrier-based Fighter Model 52.Production [serial] Number: Mitsubishi No. 4523. Assigned [to]: Nishijima, Crew Chief.

The true s/ns of the complete run of Mitsubishi-built A6M2s ranged from number 3 (403) through 806 (2806), meaning that the company turned out 804 A6M2s from December 1939 through June 1942. (Of this number, several were completed as prototypes for later versions and may have been reserialed.) To an uninformed person having access to the starting and finishing s/ns, it would have appeared that Mitsubishi had produced 2,404 A6M2 airframes (403 through 2806), exactly the kind of misconception the Japanese wanted.

From the Japanese standpoint, all of these aircraft could be referred to by their true s/ns or by their coded s/ns, as just explained. For example, in the A6M2 maintenance and handling manuals, Japanese Navy manual writers cited the true s/ns. In operational and administrative documents, the reader would find either true or coded s/ns being quoted.

Nakajima A6M2 Serial Numbers

The Nakajima-built Zeros had three-digit, four-digit, and as yet unknown in 1942, two- and five-digit s/ns. But regardless of the number of digits, the intelligence team asserted that the first digit once again could be ignored, leaving the true s/n in view. They applied this theory to the few numbers they knew, and the dates of assembly seemed to make sense.

Although seemingly unimportant, the gnawing question remained as to what system was being used in selecting the first, yet false digit. In time, the intelligence team discovered that the code digits vary from 1 to 9 according to what numeral was in the *tens* position of true s/ns from 10 and above, and that the sum of the code digit and the *tens* digit must equal 10 or 1. Thus, the allowable combinations were 9-1, 8-2, 7-3, 6-4, 5-5, 4-6, 3-7, 2-8, 1-9, and 1-0. Typical serials with this rule looked like 1190 (1+9=10), 7234 (7+3=10), and 1503 (1+0=1). This became known as the ten-cycle system.

There were exceptions. The code digit would always be 1 if the true serial were less than 10; for example, 13 or 18. (Nakajima used this same system on the A6M2, the A6M2-N, and all other aircraft they built for the Navy.)

Production Summary by Serial Number by James F. Lansdale

Up to this point, "contractor number" (c/n) has not been mentioned, but it does have a bearing on the following charts. Therefore, we must clarify by defining both terms. "Serial number" refers to the visible number by which the user (JNAF) identifies the airplane.

"Contractor number" (c/n) refers to the number that has been assigned by the manufacturer. (In this discussion, the Navy s/n is created by adding a prefix to the contractor number.)

Mitsubishi A6M1 and A6M2 Production and Serials

Model and Type	No. Built
C/N and S/N	
A6M1/12-Shi	2

c/ns 1–2; s/ns 201 and 302

A6M2/12-Shi	18

c/ns 3–20; s/ns 403, 504, 605, 706, 807, 908, 209, 310, 411, 512, 613, 714, 815, 916, 217, 318, 419, 520

A6M2/Model 11	46

c/ns 21–66; s/ns encoded using the eight-cycle coding system: 621, 722, 823, 924, 225, 326, 427, and so on

A6M2/Model 21	33

c/ns 67–99; s/ns encoded using the eight-cycle coding system: 467, 568, 669, 770, 871, 972, 273, and so on

	707

c/ns 100–806; s/ns encoded using the following false prefixes (five-cycle coding system):

False prefix	Last digit of c/n
1	0 or 5
2	1 or 6
3	2 or 7
4	3 or 8
5	4 or 9

For example, aircraft c/ns 100–109 were serialed 1100, 2101, 3102, 4103, 5104, 1105, 2106, 3107, 4108, 5109, and so on

Total A6M1 & A6M2	**806**

Mitsubishi A6M3 through A6M8 Production and Serials

Model and Type	No. Built	S/N
A6M3 Model 32	343	3001–3343
A6M3 Model 22	560	3344–3903
A6M5 Model 52	747	3904–4650
A6M5 Model 52a	391	4651–5041
A6M5 Model 52b	470	5042–5511
A6M5 Model 52c	}	}
A6M7 Model 62	} 523	}
A6M7 Model 63	}	} 5512–6037
A6M6 Model 53c	1	}
A6M8 Model 54c	2	}
Total	3,037	

Total Mitsubishi Zero Production: 3,843

Nakajima Zero Production and Serial Numbers

Model and Type	No. Built	S/N*
A6M2 Model 21	2,628	X1–X2628
A6M2-N	254	X1–X254
A6M5 Model 52	}	
A6M7 Model 62	} 3,573	X1–X3573
A6M7 Model 63	}	
Total	6,455	

Note: X represents a false prefix number.
*Includes c/n and s/n.

Nakajima Zero False Prefixes and Serial Numbers

Nakajima encoded their contractor number on all aircraft produced for the JNAF using the following serial system. The first nine aircraft of each major variant were serialed 11 through 19. Subsequent aircraft contractor numbers were prefixed as follows:

False Prefix (X)	Serial/Contractor Numbers
9 when c/n ended in 10-19	(910-919, 9110-9119, 9210-9219, and so on)
8 when c/n ended in 20-29	(820-829, 8120-8129, 8220-8229, and so on)
7 when c/n ended in 30-39	(730-739, 7130-7139, 7230-7239, and so on)
6 when c/n ended in 40-49	(640-649, 6140-6149, 6240-6249, and so on)
5 when c/n ended in 50-59	(550-559, 5150-5159, 5250-5259, and so on)
4 when c/n ended in 60-69	(460-469, 4160-4169, 4260-4269, and so on)
3 when c/n ended in 70-79	(370-379, 3170-3179, 3270-3279, and so on)
2 when c/n ended in 80-89	(280-289, 2180-2189, 2280-2289, and so on)
1 when c/n ended in 90-99	(190-199, 1190-1199, 1290-1299, and so on)
1 when c/n ended in 00-09	(1100-1109, 1200-1209, and so on)

Total Zero Production of all Types

Model and Type	No. Built
Mitsubishi A6M	3,843
Nakajima A6M	6,201
A6M2-N	254
21st NAD A6M2-K	238
Hitachi A6M2-K	279
Total	**10,815**

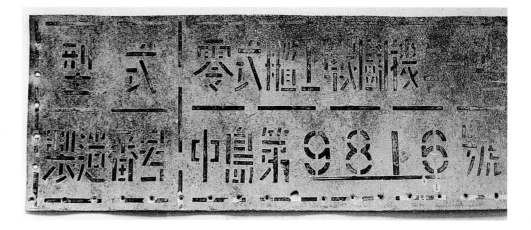

This photo shows two lines from the fuselage stencil of a Nakajima-built Zero 21. The two other lines were on the skin panel attached below this section, and are not shown. Unlike Mitsubishi, Nakajima persisted in using the four-line stencil even though no production dates appeared after November 1942. Based upon production rate, Nakajima completed this aircraft during March 1943. The entries, including the missing third and fourth lines, are as follows:
Model-type: Type Zero Carrier-based Fighter Model 21.
Production [serial] Number: Nakajima No. 9816.
Production Date: (left blank)
Assigned [to]: (left blank)
Charles Darby via James F. Lansdale

Chapter 13

The Survivors

Amazingly, the population of surviving Zeros appears to grow with each passing year. For nearly 20 years following the end of the war, evidence of the Zero's existence seemed limited to the one in storage at the National Air and Space Museum, two in the hands of the Planes of Fame in California, and the A6M7 on outdoor exhibit at NAS Willow Grove, Pennsylvania. A few derelicts can be found elsewhere.

In the years that followed, interest began to increase not only for these few lone survivors, but for those crashed and remaining parts that could be found on the Pacific islands. Recovery of these corroding hulks became popular not only by museums, but in greater number by private collectors. Many have been restored for exhibits, and two or

Friend and foe at the National Museum of Naval Aviation are this Grumman FM-2 and Nakajima-built A6M2 (s/n 5450).

three have been restored to flying condition. Today, more than 30 Zeros remain. We are fortunate in having these examples of this legendary aircraft to admire, study, and appreciate for the qualities that it contained as a fighting aircraft of that time period.

For those who are interested in seeing these Zero survivors that are in museums and in private hands, here is a directory listing the aircraft and the locations at which they can be found, as of late 1993.

Key describing condition:
A—Complete and exhibit aircraft
B—All basic components, but not assembled
C—Some basic components, or needing major restoration
F—Flyable
R—Replica
*—S/n suspect
**—First numbers are from major components, second numbers are aircraft data plates

The Mitsubishi A6M5 (s/n 4340) that is on exhibit at the National Air and Space Museum, Washington, D.C.

To maintain factory tradition, Mitsubishi restored this A6M5a (s/n 4708) which is kept at their Nagoya Plant. T. Kanamura

Model/Type	Tail Mark	S/n	Cond.	Holder & Address
A6M2	BII-124	**5349**	C	Darwin Aviation Museum, PO Box 38037, Winnellie, NT, 0821, Australia
A6M2 Nakajima	EII-102	**5356***	F	Confederate Air Force, Midland International Airport, Midland, TX, 79711
A6M2 Nakajima	EII-140 (USMC)	**5450***	A	National Museum of Naval Aviation, Naval Air Station Pensacola, FL, 32508
A6M2		**5784**	A	Australian War Memorial, PO Box 305, Canberra City, A.C.T. 2601, Australia
A6M2 Nakajima.		**91518**	C	Nobuo Harada, 3-16-11 Kugahara, Ohta, Tokyo, Japan
A6M2 Nakajima		**51553**	B	US Air Force Museum, Wright-Patterson AFB, Dayton, OH, 45433
A6M2 Nakajima		**92717***	C	Nobuo Harada, 3-16-11 Kugahara, Ohta, Tokyo, Japan
A6M2	53-122		A	National Science Museum, 7-20 Uneo-Koen, Taito-ku, Tokyo 110, Japan
A6M2			B	Maimaluau, New Ireland
A6M2			C	Robert Diemert, Carmen, Manitoba, Canada
A6M3 Model 32	Y2-128		A	Air and Space Museum, Nagoya Airport Building, Toyoyama-cho, Nishikasugai-gun, Aichi Prefecture 480-02, Japan
A6M3 Model 32	S-128/Y2-128	**3148/3318****	C	John and Tom Sterling, 1081 N. Mitchell, Boise, ID, 83704
A6M3 Model 22	Y2-176	**3489/3685****	C	John and Tom Sterling, 1081 N. Mitchell, Boise, ID, 83704
A6M3 Model 22	2-182	**3844**	A	Auckland Institute and Museum, The Domain, Parnell, Auckland, New Zealand
A6M3 Model 22			C	Museum of Flying, 2772 Donald Douglas Loop N., Santa Monica, CA, 90405
A6M5	3-108	**4043**	C	Weeks Air Museum, 14710 SW, 128th Street, Miami, FL, 33186
A6M5	30-1153		A	Museum Pusat Tni-Au, Dirgantara Mandala, Lanud Adisutjipto, Yogyakarta 55002, Indonesia
A6M5		**4241**	A	Nobuo, Harada, 3-16-11 Kugahara, Ohta, Tokyo, Japan
A6M5	61-131	**4340**	A	National Air and Space Museum, Smithsonian Institution, Washington, DC, 20560
A6M5 Nakajima		**5350**	C	R. D. Wittington, World Jet, 1020 NW 62nd St., Ft. Lauderdale, FL, 33309
A6M5 Nakajima	61-120	**5357**	F	Planes of Fame, Chino Airport, 7000 Merrill Avenue, Chino, CA, 91710
A6M5	HK-102	**4400***	A	Planes of Fame, Chino Airport, 7000 Merrill Avenue, Chino, CA, 91710
A6M5 Nakajima		**1493***	C	Nobuo Harada, 3-16-11 Kugahara, Ohta, Tokyo, Japan
A6M5a	43-188	**4685**	A	Hamamatsu AB Collection, O, Nishiyama-chou, Hamamatsu-cho, Shizuoka Prefecture 432, Japan
A6M5a		**4708**	A	Mitsubishi Heavy Industry, Komaki South Plant, Nagoya, Japan
A6M5 (cockpit only)	BI-05		C	Imperial War Museum, Lambeth Road, London SE1 6HZ, England
A6M5			B	Coastwatchers War Memorial, Rabaul, New Britain, Papua New Guinea
A6M5			B	Military Museum of the Chinese People's Revolution, 9 Fuxing Lu, Beijing, China
A6M5			R	Zero Hangar Visitor Center, Marine Corps Air Station Iwakuni, Yamaguchi Prefecture, Japan
A6M5c			A	Kanoya Air Base, Kyushu, Japan
A6M7			C	Kamikaze Museum, PO Box 897-03, Chiran, Kagoshima Prefecture, Japan
A6M7 Nakajima (Lent from NASM)		**23186**	A	San Diego Aerospace Museum, 2001 Pan American Plaza, Balboa Park, San Diego, CA
A6M7	210-118B		A	Kyoto-Arashiyama Museum, 32-22 Tsukurimuchi-cho, Sagatenryu-ji, Ukyo-ku, Kyoto, Japan

Note: True s/ns are in boldface. Subtract 3000 from the Mitsubishi A6M5 serials to get their true s/ns.

A most unusual exhibit. This A6M5a was recovered from Teuchi Harbor near Kagoshima and exhibited as found at the Kamikaze Museum, Kyushu

Appendix A

Zero Fighter Technical Data

Zero Dimensions

Main Dimensions

	Model 21 (Source 1)	Model 32 (Source 2)	Model 52 (Source 3)
Wingspan	39' 4-7/16"	36' 2-1/4"	36' 1-1/16"
Length, level	29' 8"	29' 9"	29' 11-3/32"
Length, three-point			29' 2-19/32"
Height, level		9' 2"	11' 6-5/32"
Height, three-point			11' 8-1/2"
Three-point (landing)			12.5deg

Propeller

Model			Sumitomo
Diameter	9' 6"	10' 3"	10' 1/16"
Pitch range	25–45deg	29–49deg	29–49deg
Weight			320.3lb

Main Wing

Span	39' 4-7/16	36' 2-1/4	36' 1-1/16
Chord at fuselage CL	8' 3"	8' 3"	8' 2-7/16"
Chord 20" from CL		8' 1"	
Chord thickness at CL		8-1/4"	
Chord thickness at tip		4-1/8"	
Chord, MAC		6' 4.8"	6' 7-31/32"
Chord at tip	4' 1-1/2"	4' 1-1/4"	
Chord thickness at tip		4-1/8"	
Surface area	228.4sq-ft	232sq-ft	229.59sq-ft
Angle of incidence			
Root			2deg
Tip			0.5deg
Dihedral angle		6.5 at 30% chord	5.71deg
Aspect ratio	6.75	5.5	
Airfoil			
Root (NACA)	2315	2315	
Tip (NACA)	3309	3309	
Taper ratio		44	
Skin		0.022–0.028"	

Wing Flaps

Width	5' 4"	5' 3-3/4"	5' 10-31/32"
Chord, inboard	1' 6"		1' 8"
Chord, outboard	1' 3"		1' 4-1/2"
Surface area		16.44sq-ft	8.93sq-ft (x2)
Angle of movement			60deg

Ailerons

Width	10' 10"	9' 7-5/8"	9' 4-27/32"
Chord			1' 3-29/32"
Area		20.2sq-ft	15.95sq-ft (x2)
Angle of setting			0deg 10min
Chord, inboard	16-1/2"		
Chord, outboard	8"		
Angle of movement			
Up	28deg		
Down	20deg		

Horizontal Stabilizer

Span	15' 5"	15' 5"	15' 5-1/32"
Chord, root			4' 8-1/2"
Chord, mean		3'	
Surface area			16.06sq-ft (x2)
Stabilizer area, total		40.84sq-ft	
Horizontal tail area		51.63sq-ft	
Angle of setting			0deg 10min
Airfoil, root (NACA)		0000-64 (approx.)	
Airfoil, tip (NACA)		0010	
Aspect ratio		5.7	
Taper ratio		0.439	
Skin		0.018–0.025"	

Vertical Stabilizer

Height from fuselage CL		4' 6"	5' 7-23/32"
Surface area		7.92sq-ft	9.96sq-ft
Angle of setting			0deg

Elevator

Span			13' 3"
Chord			1' 2"
Surface area		10.85sq-ft	5.29x2sq-ft
Angle of movement			
Up	26deg		27deg
Down	22deg		21.5deg
Balance		11.35%	
Trim tab area		1.19sq-ft	

Rudder

Height		4' 6"	4' 5-1/2"
Height from fuselage CL			5' 7-23/32"
Chord			2' 7"

Surface area		7.7sq-ft	7.45sq-ft
Angle of movement			
Left	30deg		33deg
Right	37deg		33deg
Forward balance		0.7sq-ft	
Trim tab area		0.065sq-ft	
Balance		9.64%	
Fuselage			
Length			23' 1"
Width			3' 6-11/16"
Height			5' 4-1/32"
Skin thickness	0.021"	0.018–0.048"	
Main Wheels			
Diameter	23.6"		23.62"
Width	6.9"		6.88"
Tire pressure			50lb
Tire size		23x6.9	
Tread			11' 5-13/16"
Tire size	600x175		
Tail Wheel			
Diameter			5.90"
Width			2.95"
Tire pressure			Solid
Weight (lb)			
Empty	3,770	3,913	4,130
Gross	5,555	5,155	5,920
Overload		6,331	6,510
Normal load		5,750	6,049.2
Useful load	1,430		1,872.9
Permissible overload			6,818.1
Propeller			320.3
Wing load (lb/sq-ft)	24.3**	21.3	25.8
Power load (lb/hp)		5.42	
Takeoff			5.31
Normal			6.88
Military			6.14
Wheel and tire		28	
C.G. M.A.C.		31%	

Fuel Capacity (US gallons)

Wing tanks	51.51x2	55.48x2	69.75x2
Fuselage tank	38.31	15.8	15.8
Auxiliary tank*	87.18	87.18	87.18
Total fuel	228.51	213.94	242.44
Oil capacity	15.32	13.73	13.73

Note:

*Drop tanks with varying capacities were also used, such as the 84gal tank.

**For normal gross weight-not specific for other two models.

***JICPOA Item 5981. See Appendix C.

Sources:

The primary sources of technical data, listed below, are considered to contain the most accurate information available. Much data is missing for specific models, and although it *may* be the same for all Zero models, it is not assumed so.

Source 1: *Preliminary Measurements of Flying Qualities of the Japanese Mitsubishi Company Pursuit Airplane,* W. H. Phillips, Langley Memorial Aeronautical Laboratory, NACA [Akutan Zero], May 5, 1943 (and augmented by other sources).

Source 2: "Design Analysis of Zeke 32," *Aviation Magazine,* May 1945, John Foster, Jr. American study of captured aircraft from TAIC, Australia.

Source 3: Technical Air Intelligence Center Summary #32, "Evolution of Zeke," June 1945.

Appendix B

A6M2-N Technical Data

A6M2-N Technical Data

With the exception of the float alighting system, the A6M2-N Rufe airframe is basically the same as the A6M2 Zero. All Rufes were manufactured by Nakajima Aircraft Company Ltd.

Primary source for the following data (converted from metric) is from the *Encyclopedia of Japanese Aircraft, Vol. 5, Nakajima Aircraft,* by Tadashi Nozawa and Takashi Iwata. Tokyo: Shuppan-Kyolo, 1983.

Dimensions–

Wing Span: 39ft 4–7/16in
Length: 33ft 1–5/8in
Height: 14ft 1–5/16in
Wing Area: 248 sq ft

Weights

Empty: 4,145lb
Load: 1,188lb
Normal: 5,920lb
Overload: 6,436lb
Wing loading: 22.5lb/sq ft
Power loading: 5.7lb/hp

Equipment

Engine: Nakajima Sakae 12
Armament: 7.7mm mg x 2
20mm cannon x 2
30–60kg bomb x 2

Fuel Capacity

Fuselage and wing tanks: 136.9USgal
Float tank: 85.8USgal
Total: 222.6USgal
Oil tank: 15.3USgal

Performance

Top speed: 235kt at 16,406ft
Best cruise: 160kt at 13,124ft
Landing speed: 61kt
Climb to 9,843ft: 3min 57sec
Climb to 16,405ft: 6min 43sec
Service Ceiling: 32,022ft
Maximum Ceiling: 32,810ft
Normal range: 620nm
Maximum range: 962nm
Maximum endurance: 6hr

Appendix C

Zero Flight Performance

Zero Flight Performance

The following is a translation of a captured Japanese document, dated October 1943, captured on Kwajalein Atoll, and received by Joint Intelligence Center, Pacific Ocean Areas (JICPOA) February 19, 1944. It was then published as *JICPOA Item #5981,* using knots and metric system. Conversion from meters to feet is shown here.

	Model 21	**Model 22**	**Model 32**	**Model 52**
Maximum Speed (kt)/optimum altitude (ft)				
Low Blower	275/14,436	281/10,663	280/11,319	282/10,663
High Blower	N/A	292/19,357	290/20,178	294/19,357
(Blower shift altitude was 15,420ft)				
Rate of Climb to 6,000m (19,686ft)	7min 27 sec	7min 19sec	7min 5sec	7min 27sec
Takeoff distance				
No wind, no flaps	650ft	614ft	660ft	630ft
23.3kt wind, no flaps	269ft	233ft	279ft	272ft
Overload condition				
No wind, 20 deg flaps		732ft	843ft	824ft
23.3kt wind, 20deg flap		302ft	394ft	361ft
Fuel Consumption (US gallons per hour)				
At 180kt	16.4		21.98	
At 190kt	24.04		24.43	
At 200kt	26.15		26.97	
At max rated hp	91.14		114.92	
Oil consumption (US gallons per hour)	1.42	0.92	0.92	0.92
Flying range with combat time				
After 30min	774nm	800nm	562nm	
After 20min	900nm	962nm	727nm	
After 10min	1025nm	1110nm	877nm	

Appendix D

Zero Flight Data

Parameter	Model 21 (Source 1)	Model 32 (Source 2)	Model 52 (Source 3)
Maximum Speed (kt)			
Sea level	234	243	
5,000	249	257	
10,000	264	269	
15,000		264	
20,000	279	264	305
25,000	274	260	
30,000	266	255	
Speed Limitations (kt IAS)			
Maximum	340	360	360
Landing gear down	130	130	130
Flap extension	120	120	120
Landing Speed (kt)			
Glide	74		65–69
Touchdown	48		56–61
Stall Speed (kt)			
Gear up, power on	64		70
Gear up, power off	68	74	74
Gear down, power on	53	57	57
Gear down, power off	60	68	68
Rate of Climb (fpm)			
Sea level	2,750	3,260	
5,000		3,060	
7,000		2,980	
10,000		2,460	
15,000	2,380	2,180	
20,000	1,810	1,650	
25,000		1,120	
30,000	850	600	
Service Ceiling	38,500	38,800	38,520

Sources

Source 1: *Information Intelligence Summary No. 85,* Intelligence Service, US Army Air Forces, December 1942.

Source 2: *Performance Flight Test on a Japanese Hamp, AAF No. EB-201, Wright Field, March 1944,* document IP 2369.

Source 3: Various sources

Appendix E

Type 99 Machine Gun Technical Data

Type 99 Machine Gun Technical Data

Designation	Mk.1 Model 3	Mk.2 Model 3	Mk.2 Model 4	Mk.2 Model 5
Caliber (mm)	20	20	20	20
Weight of Round (gram/lb)	123/0.271	123/0.271	123/0.271	123/0.271
Muzzle velocity (m/sec; ft/sec)	600/1,968	750/2,460	750/2,460	760/2,493
Rounds fired per minute.	520	490	500	750
Weight (kg/lb)	23.2/51.14	33.5/73.85	37.57/82.82	38.5/84.87
Length (mm/in)	1,331/52.45	1,890/74.85	1,890/74.85	1,855/73.1
Barrel (mm/in)	812/31.96	1,250/49.25	1,250/49.25	1,250/49.25
Feed type	Magazine	Magazine	Belt	Belt
Round cap.	60 rounds	100 rounds		
Zero models	12-*Shi,* 11, 21, 32, ** 22,	22a, 52	52a, 52b, 52c, 53c, 63, 54c	64*

*Probable but uncomfirmed installation.

**From airframe #4, changed from 60-round magazine to 100-round magazine per gun. True for Nakajima Model 21 production after July 1942

Sources:

Kawakami, Yohei, Lt. Cmdr. *General View of Japanese Naval Aeronautical Engineering,* Vol. II, Chapter 2—Airborne Gunnery Weapon, Tokyo: Nippon Suppan Kyodo K.K., 1955.

Ikari, Yoshiro. *Naval Air Technical Arsenal,* Tokyo: K.K. Kojinsha, 1989.

Mitsubishi A6M Production 1939–1945

Mitsubishi A6M Production 1939–1945
Source: US Strategic Bombing Survey

Fiscal Year Type/Model	Apr	May	Jun	Jul	Aug	Sep	Oct	Nov	Dec	Jan	Feb	Mar	FY Total
1938/39													
A6M1												1*	1
1939/40													
A6M1							1						1
A6M2/Mo.11									1	1	1	1	4
1940/41													
A6M2/Mo.11	1	4	3	9	8	9	19	7					60
A6M2/Mo.21								16	19	23	23	30	111
1941/42													
A6M2/Mo.21	27	30	25	24	30	33	43	52	60	59	58	55	496
A6M3/Mo.32			1	1						1			3†
1942/43													
A6M2/Mo.21	54	58	21										133
A6M3/Mo.32			24	46	51	64	65	67	23				340
A6M3/Mo.22									46	68	69	73	256
1943/44													
A6M3/Mo.22	73	73	72	77	9								304
A6M5			1		76	93	105	109	130	125	108		747
A6M5a								1			7	105	113
1944/45													
A6M5a	108	95	75										278
A6M5b	1		25	115	135	134	60						470
A6M5c and A6M7						1	85	114	62	35	59	40	396
A6M6c								1					1
1945													
A6M5c/A6M7	36	37	23	15	16‡								127
A6M8	1	1											2

Total: 3,843

Notes: *Does not include one airframe for static vibration and stress tests.

†"Production figures for prototypes cannot always be recognized in the over-all Mitsubishi production figures and, in years prior to 1944, a few are doubtless counted as regular production" (*USSBS Studies, Pacific War*, Report 16, p.75)

‡The same source shows that fifty-two A6M7s were produced by Mitsubishi during August 1945, fifty-one being produced at the Mie plant and one at the Omi plant. Evidence indicates that the fifty-one reported from the Mie plant is due to an error in number transposition. The corrected figures used above would be fifteen produced at Mie and one at Omi. The resulting total, therefore, is 16. In addition, *Japanese Monograph No. 174: Outline of Naval Armament and Preparations for War, Part VI,* published by the Military History Section Special Staff, Japanese Research Division, U.S. Army Hq, Far East Command, in 1952, lists a total of 101 Zeros that were produced by Nakajima and Mitsubishi during August 1945. By deducting the eighty-five Zeros known to have been produced by Nakajima during that month, the resulting number of sixteen is shown to be the Mitsubishi output. Indirect evidence is also available. The production figures for Mitsubishi for the previous months show declining production capacity, with only fifteen Zeros being produced during July. It is highly unlikely that Mitsubishi could have been able to produce the higher number of fifty-two at that stage of the war.)

Nakajima A6M Production 1941–1945

Nakajima A6M Production 1941–1945
Source: **US Strategic Bombing Survey**

Fiscal Year / Type	Apr	May	Jun	Jul	Aug	Sep	Oct	Nov	Dec	Jan	Feb	Mar	FY Total
1941/42													
A6M2								1	(5)	19	(21)	(23)	(69)
A6M2-N									(1)		(1)	(2)	(4)
1942/43													
A6M2	22	28	29	41	52	62	72	80	96	89	100	112	783
A6M2-N	9	8	5	11	13	13	16	19	22	21	19	21	177
1943/44													
A6M2	120	126	132	146	156	170	182	202	225	238	79		1776
A6M2-N	24	22	20	7		*							73*
A6M5											75	271	346
1944/45													
A6M5	230	232	200	163	232	245	194	109	206	216	108	207	2,342
1945													
A6M5/A6M7	230	247	185	138	85								885

Nakajima Production Totals
A6M2: 2,628
A6M2-N: 254
A6M5/A6M7: 3,573

Total: 6,455

Notes: Numbers in parentheses indicate corrections based upon calculations made from known data plates, logs, or other documentary evidence. Mathematical or typographical errors have also been corrected.
*An apparent bookkeeping or typographical error entered in the September column for the A6M2-N, doubled its production for FY 1943/44. With this correction, previously recorded quantities are reduced by seventy-three.

Hitachi A6M Production 1944–1945

Hitachi A6M Production 1944–1945
Source: US Strategic Bombing Survey

Fiscal Year Type/Model	Apr	May	Jun	Jul	Aug	Sep	Oct	Nov	Dec	Jan	Feb	Mar	FY Total
1944/45 A6M2-K*		2	7	15	19	10	19	27	25	23	8	34†	189
1945 A6M2-K*	21	31	23	15									90

Total: 279

Notes: *Report lists A6M5-K but this is believed to be in error. Only a few of this variant were built.
†First of seven Hitachi A6M5-Ks included in this figure; Francillon, *Japanese Aircraft of the Pacific War*, p.398.

21st Naval Air Depot A6M Production 1943–1944

21st Naval Air Depot A6M Production 1943–1944
Source: US Strategic Bombing Survey

Fiscal Year Type/Model	Apr	May	Jun	Jul	Aug	Sep	Oct	Nov	Dec	Jan	Feb	Mar	FY Total
1942/43 A6M2-K								(1)*		4	5	6	15
1943/44 A6M2-K	8	8	8	10	10	12	12	12	15	12	16	17	140
1944/45 A6M2-K	18	15	16	15	10†	5	4						83

Total: 238

Notes: *Prototype reported by Francillon, *Japanese Aircraft of the Pacific War*, possibly from components previously accounted for.
†Production of A6M5-K version began. Quantity unknown. Ibid.
Source: US Strategic Bombing Survey

Glossary

Babs: Mitsubishi Navy Type 98 Command Reconnaissance Plane (C5M)

Betty: Mitsubishi Navy Type 1 Attack Bomber (G4M)

BuAir: See *Kaigun Koku Hombu*

BuShip: See *Kaigun Kanse Hombu*

Claude: Mitsubishi Navy Type 96 Carrier Fighter (A5M)

Chutai: Flight within a squadron equivalent; eight or nine aircraft

Daitai: Squadron equivalent; 18–27 aircraft (two or more *Chutai*)

Hikota: Acronym for *Hikoki-Tai;* aircraft force, air complement, or air echelon (see *Sentoki-Tai*)

JAAF: Japanese Army Air Force

JICPOA: Joint Intelligence Center, Pacific Ocean Areas (Allied)

JNAF: Japanese Naval Air Force

Kaigun Kanse Hombu: Naval Bureau of Ships (see BuShip)

Kaigun Koku-Gijutsu-Sho: Naval Air Technical Arsenal, acronym, *Kugisho*

Kaigun Koku Hombu: Naval Bureau of Aeronautics; similar to US Naval Bureau of Aeronautics (BuAir)

Kanjo: Carrier-based, as "aboard a warship"

Kate: Nakajima Navy Type 97 Carrier Attack Bomber (B5N)

Ki, as in *Ki-27: Kitai,* meaning airframe

Kokutai: Air group, land-based

Kugisho: Acronym for *Kaigun Koku-Gijutsu-Sho* (Naval Technical Air Arsenal), located at Yokosuka; time period April 1, 1939 to February 15, 1945

Nell: Mitsubishi Navy Type 96 Attack Bomber (G3M)

Rei: Zero

Sen, or *Sentoki:* Fighter

Sentoki-Tai: Fighter Force

ShiShisaku Seizo: meaning trial manufacture

Showa: Time period, 1926–1989

Shiki: Type, as in name of aircraft

SWPA: Southwest Pacific Area, an Allied operational term identifying area of jurisdiction

Taisho: Time period, 1919–1926

Yokosuka Kaigun Kokutai: Yokosuka Naval Air Group

Bibliography

Abe, Shoji. *Combat Record of Rei-sen Model 52.* Tokyo: Bunrindo Famous Aircraft of the World, No. 54, 1974.

Akira, Yoshimura. *Rei-shiki Sentoki.* 1968. (Japanese language)

Caidin, Martin. *Zero Fighter.* New York: Ballantine, 1970.

Francillon, Rene J. *Japanese Aircraft of the Pacific War.* New York: Funk & Wagnalls, 1970.

Francillon, Rene J. *The Mitsubishi A6M2 Zero-Sen.* Leatherhead, Surrey, England: Profile Publications, 1966.

Francillon, Rene J. *The Mitsubishi A6M3 Zero-Sen.* Leatherhead, Surrey, England: Profile Publications, 1967.

Hata, Ikuhiko, and Yasuho Isawa. *Japanese Naval Aces and Fighter Units in World War II.* Annapolis, Maryland: Naval Institute Press, 1989.

Horikoshi, Jiro. *Eagles of Mitsubishi.* University of Washington Press, 1981.

Ikari, Yoshiro. *Naval Air Technical Arsenal,* Tokyo: KK Kojinsha, 1989.

Iwata, Takashi. *Type Rei Carrier Fighter, Model 11-22.* Tokyo: Bunrindo Famous Aircraft of the World, No. 10, 1974.

Kawakami, Yohei, Lt. Comdr. *General View of Japanese Naval Aeronautical Engineering,* Vol. II, Chapter 2, Airborne Gunnery Weapon, Tokyo: Nippon Suppan Kyodo KK, 1955.

Maru Editorial Staff. *Photo Album of Rei-sen,* Tokyo: Kojinsha KK, revised 1976.

Mikesh, Robert C. *Zero Fighter.* New York: Crown, 1981.

Nakagawa, Ryoichi, and Soutaro Mizutani. *History of Nakajima Aero-Engines.* Tokyo, 1985.

Nohara, Shigeru. *Mitsubishi A6M Zero Fighter.* Aero Detail 7. Tokyo: Dai Nippon Kaiga Company, Ltd., 1993.

Nozawa, Tadashi, and Takashi Iwata. *Encyclopedia of Japanese Aircraft, Vol. 5 Nakajima.* Tokyo: Shuppan-Kyodo, 1983.

Nozawa, Tadashi, and Takashi Iwata. *Encyclopedia of Japanese Aircraft, Vol. 1 Mitsubishi.* Tokyo: Shuppan-Kyodo, 1981.

Okumiya, Masatake, and Jiro Horikoshi. *Zero.* New York: Ballantine, 1956.

Okumiya, Masatake, Jiro Horikoshi, and Martin Caidin. *The Zero Fighter.* London: Cassell & Company, Ltd., 1958.

Rearden, Jim. *Cracking the Zero Mystery.* Harrisburg, PA: Stackpole, 1990.

Sakai, Saburo. *Samurai.* New York: E. P. Dutton, 1957.

Sekigawa, Eiichiro. *Japanese Military Aviation.* London: Ian Allan, 1974.

Senshi Sosho, "Hawaii Sakusen," Vol. 10 (War History Compendium Vol. 10. "The Hawaiian Operation") by War History Room, Defense Training Institute, National Defense Agency. Tokyo: Asagumo Newspaper Company, Ltd., 1967. (Japanese language)

Takagi, Kaoru. *Zero Model 21, Maru Mechanic No. 3,* Tokyo: Ushioshobo KK, 1977.

Takagi, Kaoru. *Zero Model 52, Maru Mechanic No. 4,* Tokyo: Ushioshobo KK, 1977.

US Strategic Bombing Survey, 1947:
Army Air Arsenal and Navy Air Depots
Hitachi Aircraft Company
Mitsubishi Aircraft Company
Nakajima Aircraft Company

Zero Pilots Association, *Kaigun Sentokitai-shi* (Naval Fighter Force History). Tokyo: Hara Shobo, 1987. (Japanese language)

Index